Extending and Developing Portage

Proceedings of the Fifth National Portage Conference held in Huddersfield, September 1985

Edited by
Robin Hedderly and Kath Jennings

NFER-NELSON

43453

Published by The NFER-NELSON Publishing Company Ltd.,
Darville House, 2 Oxford Road East,
Windsor, Berkshire SL4 1DF, England

and in the United States of America by

NFER-NELSON, 242 Cherry Street, Philadelphia, PA 19106 – 1906.
Tel: (215) 238 0939. Telex: 244489.

First Published 1987

Library of Congress Cataloging in Publication data

Typeset in Plantin by First Page Ltd, Watford
Printed in Great Britain by A. Wheaton & Co. Ltd, Exeter

ISBN: 0 7005 1111 3
Code: 8255 02 1

Contents

Editorial

The development of the Portage methodology in the United Kingdom continues to move on apace. An annual publication of the proceedings of the National Portage Association Conference has been one way of recording and documenting some of this progress. This year's publication, *Extending and Developing Portage*, is no exception in this endeavour but as with all previous publications it only reflects a small amount of the work that is being done and the progress that is being made up and down the country.

This last year has seen the first year's allocation of education support grant money to local education authorities for the setting up of the Portage projects. This meant for us, the Conference organizers, that as well as including innovative and exciting new ventures relating to Portage we also needed to present information at a more basic level for people who had no experience and little knowledge of the Portage methodology, techniques and the personnel involved. As a consequence the climate of the Conference turned out to be a mixture of the consolidation of existing practices and successes and the moving forward into new exciting areas.

As with all previous Conferences the success of the event was attributable for the most part to the warmth, support and optimism generated by the Conference attenders and contributors. Our thanks go to you all.

Robin Hedderly and Kath Jennings
Conference Organizers

The National Portage Association

The Association

The National Portage Association (NPA) was conceived in 1983 in response to an expressed need to have a network of people to help support the increasing number of Portage practitioners. These include home visitors, other professionals from a variety of disciplines and of course parents. The National Portage Association was formally constituted at the 1984 Liverpool Conference and the 1985 Conference celebrated the first anniversary of the formally constituted National Portage Association.

Aims

The aims of the Association are to disseminate information about Portage and to encourage developments in the service.

The Association is concerned to ensure standards of service delivery are maintained and that training is available at both basic and advanced levels. To this end the NPA maintains a register of trainers for basic workshops and is developing an advanced workshop curriculum for experienced practitioners. It has also organized specialist day courses.

It is also concerned to ensure that the Portage service is responsive to the needs of its consumers. Parents are equal partners in the NPA. It is their feedback which provides information which helps maintain high standards of service delivery. The NPA is interested in developing new strategies to enable parents to make their contribution even more effective.

Structure

The NPA is divided into regions, each of which has its elected representative on the National Executive. The organization of the region is the responsibility of the representative and his or her committee. Local enquiries should be addressed to the appropriate representative. There are three nationally organized committees with responsibility for ethical issues, information/publicity and training/monitoring. The chairperson of each is a nationally elected member of the executive. There are four executive officers and two parent representatives. Parents may stand for any position on the executive but the nominated positions ensure their representation.

Membership

Individual membership of the NPA is open to anyone who agrees with its aims and codes of practice, on payment of the annual subscription fee. Group membership is also available to services wishing to affiliate to the NPA on payment of the annual subscription fee. International membership is also open to any Portage practitioner. Information about joining the NPA can be obtained from the appropriate regional representative or from any member of the executive listed below.

Portage Post

The *Portage Post* is a quarterly publication through which members of the NPA are kept in touch with developments in the service. Members receive the *Portage Post* free of charge and others interested in the publication may apply to the Information Officer.

National Executive Members

National representatives

Chairperson:	Dee Williams, 30 Berkeley Road, Crouch End, London N8
Secretary:	Mollie White, 4 Clifton Road, Winchester, Hampshire
Treasurer:	Robin Hedderly, Oldgate House, 2 Oldgate, Huddersfield HD1 6QW
Membership Secretary:	Frances Russell, 10 Holt Park Drive, Leeds MS16 7RG

Parent representatives

Frances Russell (address as above)
Jo Cameron, 143 Elms Crescent, London SW4

Regional representatives

South West
Tim Lister, School Psychological Service, Floor 5, Arundel Towers North, Portland Terrace, Southampton SO9 4XE

South East and London
Sue Kerfoot, Barking and Dagenham School Psychological Service, Seabrook House, Shipton Close, Dagenham, Essex RM8 3QR

Midlands
Christine Clarke, County Psychological Service, 15 Sandford Street, Lichfield, Staffs

Eastern
Pam Gavin, Education Department, Shire Hall, Bury St Edmonds IP33 1RX

Northern
Kath Jennings, Child Guidance, Civic Centre, High Street, Huddersfield

Wales

Christina Evans, Psychology Department, Llanfrechfa Grange Hospital, Cwn Bran, Gwent NP44 8YN

Ireland (Acting Representative)

Roger Goodliffe, School Psychological Service, North East Education Library Board, County Hall, Galgorm Road, Bally Mena, County Antrim, Northern Ireland

Scotland (to be elected)

Please direct inquiries to the National Secretary

Committee representatives

Ethics

Sandra Stevens, 55 Henley Road, Ipswich, Suffolk IP 3SJ

Information and Publicity

R.J. Cameron, Room 235, Department of Psychology, Murray Building, Southampton University, Highfields, Southampton SO9 5NH

Training, Monitoring and Standards

Brian Daly, Psychological Service, 94 Newgate Street, Morpeth, Northumberland NE61 1BU

Contributors' Addresses

Patsy Barrow
Social Worker
City of Bradford Metropolitan Council
Directorate of Educational Services
School and Family Service
Woodbottom Centre
Otley Road
Baildon
Shipley
BD17 7HJ

Anne Blake
Senior Mistress
Foxdenton School
Foxdenton Lane
Chadderton
Oldham

R J Cameron
Tutor for Advanced Professional Training in Educational Psychology
University of Southampton
Dept of Psychology
Murray Building
Southampton
SO9 5NH

Christine Clarke (formerly Dickinson)
Senior Educational Psychologist
School Psychological Service
15 Sandford Street
Lichfield
Staffs

Maria Evans
Inspector of Special Needs
School Psychological Service
NE Area Education Office
7 Monument Hill
Weybridge
Surrey

Sheila Hallows
Health Visitor
Malvern Health Centre
Victoria Park Road
Malvern
WR14 2JY

Robin Hedderly
Principal Educational Psychologist
Kirklees Psychological Service
Oldgate House
2 Oldgate
Huddersfield
HD1 6QW

Angela Holland
Senior Clinical Psychologist
Leicestershire Health Authority
Dept of Psychology
Towers Hospital
Humberstone
Leicester
LE5 0TD

Jane Hubert
Health Care Evaluation Research Team
45/47 Salisbury Road
The University
Highfield
Southampton

Kath Jennings
Educational Psychologist
Portage Project Leader
Kirklees Psychological Service
Oldgate House
2 Oldgate
Huddersfield
HD1 6QW

Albert Kushlick
Health Care Evaluation
Research Team
45/47 Salisbury Road
The University
Highfield
Southampton

Stephanie Lorenz
Educational Psychologist
School Psychological/Child Guidance Service
Chaseley Road
Salford
M6 7DZ

Barbara McDowell
Educational Psychologist
Northampton School Psychological Service
'Springfield'
Cliftonville
Northampton
NN1 5BE

Gillian Pugh
Senior Development Officer
National Children's Bureau
8 Wakley Street
London
EC1V 7QE

Ewen Rennie
Acting Head Teacher
(seconded Educational Psychologist)
Combs Hill School
Hall Lane
Thornhill
Dewsbury
WF12 0QL

Susan Richards
Health Visitor
Malvern Health Centre
Victoria Park Road
Malvern
WR14 2JY

Joyce Scaife
Senior Clinical Psychologist
Leicestershire Health Authority
Dept of Psychology
Towers Hospital
Humberstone
Leicester
LE5 0TD

John Smith
Health Care Evaluation Research Team
45/47 Salisbury Road
The University
Highfield
Southampton

Peter Sturmey
Clinical Psychologist
Adult Unit 2
Olive Mount Hospital
Old Mill Lane
Wavertree
Liverpool 15

Paul Wiehl
Educational Psychologist
City of Bradford Metropolitan Council
Directorate of Educational Services
School and Family Service
Woodbottom Centre
Otley Road
Baildon
Shipley
BD17 7HJ

Anna Wright
Educational Psychologist
(Surrey C.C. School Psy. Service, Weybridge, Surrey)
Now working in London

Background to Portage in Kirklees and to the 1985 Portage Conference

R.G. Hedderly

The 1985 Portage Conference was organized by the Kirklees Portage service which itself is a branch of the Kirklees psychological service. Some years ago the Kirklees psychological service was approached with a request to organize the Conference in 1985. It therefore seemed appropriate to discuss something of the background to the development of Portage within the psychological service. The book is appropriately entitled *Extending and Developing Portage* and it is very pleasing to see that the concept of a Portage service which was initially applied to very young handicapped children is now being extended into other spheres of the education service. In 1985 the Kirklees psychological service was pleased to have received a further urban aid grant in order to extend and develop Portage into first and nursery schools. The submission for the grant also indicated that the Portage services would be designed for a wider range of children than had been normally considered hitherto. It was suggested that the Portage approach could also be considered for disadvantaged children and for children who had behaviour disorders. The 1985 Conference also represented an important development because it was the first Conference to be organized under the auspices of the National Portage Association. The National Portage Association (NPA) was formally constituted the year before in 1984 at the Conference held in Liverpool. A further milestone coincided with the 1985 Conference held in Kirklees because Portage was officially recognized as an important method of service delivery to young severely handicapped children. The government announced an education support grant was available to enable local education authorities to introduce a Portage scheme on the guidelines laid down by the NPA. This is covered in more detail in the introduction to the report of Sir Keith Joseph's speech to the 1985 National Portage Conference (p.75).

The Kirklees psychological service first became interested in the Portage concept as a result of one of the senior psychologists in Kirklees, John Grange, bringing to the attention of the service the work of Dr Albert Kushlick of the Health Care Evaluation Research Team which was based in Winchester. In 1976 John Grange insisted that the principal psychologist should read the Health Care Evaluation Research Team reports. He pointed out that the importance which was attached to the provision of an explicit psychological service in Kirklees was epitomized and encapsulated in the

Portage scheme. From 1974 and even before, the value of a contract 'referral' system where the psychologist specified the nature of an intervention with a child or family and evaluated precisely the progress in a defined time, had been advocated (Hedderly, 1977). The psychological service had moved into the use of a behavioural approach to teaching as a method of providing solutions to problems referred to the service. The original Health Care Evaluation Research Team reports clearly indicated that the Portage approach to providing a service for families of young handicapped children matched precisely the requirements and statements of the Kirklees psychological service for providing an explicit and thoroughly professional service.

The Kirklees psychological service decided to implement the Portage approach initially with one or two individual families. John Joyce, one of the Kirklees psychologists, was the first to undertake such a venture. He also acted as a home visitor in order to get first-hand experience. Feedback to him and through him was extremely positive and of course the approach enabled the service, in conjunction with the parents, in a way never before possible fully to evaluate and assess the child's development across all aspects of behaviour. Through John Grange the Kirklees psychological service built up a small library of material on the effectiveness of the Portage system of early education. We were also fortunate because the local Dr Barnado's Yorkshire divisional office expressed an interest in the Portage system for their own purposes. They requested a visit to Kirklees psychological service to consider the material and information that we had collected on Portage. The Kirklees psychological service operates a 'data bank' approach. This approach is discussed in more detail in Rennie and Joyce (1979) and in Hedderly (1980).

The Kirklees psychological service was very happy to encourage the Dr Barnado's organization to take advantage of our knowledge at that time. It also enabled the professional workers in the service to discuss with another organization the practical problems involved in using the method. At the time, Dr Barnado's was sufficiently impressed with the cooperation obtained from the psychological service that they offered on loan a full-time social worker, Jane Clifton, to undertake the home visiting role under the direction of one of the educational psychologists. Dr Barnado's organization suggested that they and the psychological service could explore the possibility of introducing a Portage service in conjunction. This process was also designed to enable both services to evaluate and develop staff skills. So two other educational psychologists, John Sheppard and Tiny Arora, became involved with a view to developing such a service and a pre-pilot project was set up in the north part of Kirklees. This was eventually evaluated by Cusworth (1980). For all the many reasons that are put forward in this book and have been put forward in previous publications on Portage, the professionals involved and the parents were delighted by the success of the service. The feedback that was received, particularly from the parents, was extremely positive. The concept of partnership was fully exploited in the Portage approach. The Kirklees authority in conjunction with the Kirklees area health authority at the time decided to apply for an urban aid grant to enable the Portage service to be developed throughout Kirklees. This unfortunately led to the withdrawal of Dr Barnardo's from the psychological service joint project. The Kirklees psychological service very much regretted this because of the value of having a voluntary organization involved. Dr Barnardo's made a significant contribution in making elected members and representatives on the health and social services as well as the education committees aware of the benefits to the authority and to the consumer of the Portage system. The application for an urban aid grant is discussed in a chapter by R.J. Cameron (1986). The urban aid grant enabled the Kirklees authority to set up under an educational psychologist, Ewen Rennie, the Kirklees Portage scheme.

This scheme is highly valued by both parents and other professionals in Kirklees although the initial development was not without its teething problems and many issues of the professional role were raised. Some of the issues were related to the introduction of a 'home visitor'. The initial aim of the Portage team in Kirklees was to have a multi-disciplinary approach to the role of the home visitor. It was thought that the home visitor could almost be any professional who was already visiting the home. This would include the health visitor, the speech therapist, the educational psychologist, the pre-school educational visitor or the social worker, either from social services or from the education department. The urban aid grant enabled the psychological service to allocate 15 hours a week of Ewen Rennie's time to develop the Kirklees Portage scheme. Three home visitors were recruited from a variety of professional backgrounds. One, for example, was an experienced infant teacher, whilst another home visitor had a background in nursery nursing. Since the initial introduction of the Kirklees Portage scheme, the service has developed from strength to strength. There have been a number of evaluations of the service and some reference is made to this later on in this book.

In 1983 Kath Jennings was appointed as an educational psychologist with the Kirklees authority and she took over the Portage scheme. One of the first tasks that she discovered she had to undertake was the organization of the 1985 Portage Conference. With this task she was ably assisted by the Portage home visitors, Carolyn Charlesworth, Margaret Wadsworth, Christine Sykes and Sue Hirst. As the Conference organization became more onerous we were very fortunate to have the services of Ruth Horsfall who undertook all the administrative work and Dorothy Hargate, the Portage secretary, who dealt with much of the typing. The Kirklees education committee also gave their support and indeed the chairman of the education committee was good enough to open the Conference. It is appropriate in this chapter to express our appreciation of the large number of other people involved in the Portage scheme, not the least being the remainder of the Kirklees psychological service. Although many were not directly involved they have encouraged us and enabled the project to go ahead. Appreciation should also be extended to the Kirklees education special services section and to all the other people involved in the Kirklees education department and in social services and the health authority who have assisted in one way or another the development of both the Portage service and the psychological service. One aspect which perhaps is an indication of the success of the Portage scheme is the fact that so many of the Portage parents attended the Conference. The Kirklees psychological service is certainly grateful for their support.

This therefore summarizes the background to the development of Portage in Kirklees and to the instigation and organization of the 1985 Portage Conference. The theme of the Conference was extending and developing Portage. The 1981 Education Act encourages professional staff to report fully on all aspects of any assessment of a child with special educational difficulties. It also encourages professionals to work with parents as partners. The Portage system enables this to be done. The professional in direct contact with the parent has very clear ideas of what their involvement will mean and also has very clear ideas of whether it will be, or has been, successful. This concept could usefully be applied to a wider group of children than hitherto, to a wider age range and to a wider curriculum within the education service. In one way or another the following chapters illustrate an area of extension or development. All these things are very encouraging for people who are working with Portage. The very fact that there is now a National Portage Association which is financially viable and officially recognized as being a source of expertise is also encouraging. It is this author's view that all caring services could be more efficiently delivered on the Portage model and one hopes that politicians and administrators will consider the Portage system when planning new services. The development of the Portage system in Kirklees has not been without its difficulties, but it has achieved a certain measure of success and the Kirklees psychological service is looking forward with great interest to the new project entitled 'Portex'. This is certainly not an indication that Portage is on the way out but rather an indication that it is ripe for extension and development and it is to be hoped that the Kirklees psychological service's five-year project will be a major force in helping this development achieve beneficial outcomes for a wider group of children and for the education service generally.

The Role of Portage in Curricular Provision

Anne Blake

An introduction to Portage

The Portage scheme brings the teaching techniques of behavioural psychology to parents, teachers and other people who spend considerable periods of time in contact with handicapped children. The Portage model is a home training system which directly involves parents in the education of their children.

The basis of the teaching system is the Curriculum Guide (Bluma *et al.*, 1976) which comprises:

(i) a developmental checklist which lists 'sequential' behaviours from birth to five years;

(ii) a set of curriculum cards to match each of the behaviours on the checklist. Each card includes a description of the skill and suggests materials and curriculum ideas for teaching it.

The checklist and curriculum cards are colour coded and divided into five developmental areas:

self help
motor
socialization
language
cognitive

(In addition, there is a section on infant stimulation which covers all five areas for teaching infants from birth to four months.)

Initial completion of the checklist helps to identify the behaviours that the child exhibits in the five developmental areas. This provides an initial baseline and information which helps advisor and parent to select a suitable skill to teach the child.

The Portage curriculum cards provide specific teaching suggestions for each objective on the behavioural checklist. These interventions are first modelled by the teacher/adviser while the parent watches. The parent then practises the teaching method with the adviser still present to give advice if necessary.

Teaching suggestions are clearly written down on a Portage activity chart with clear directions to enable parents to teach their handicapped child new skills and to record the results of the teaching effort. The criteria for writing activity charts are very precise and steps on the curriculum cards so clear and well-graded 'that the outcome is almost doomed to success' and 'most projects report success at a level of 80-95% in teaching the skills which they wish the child to acquire' (Cameron, 1979).

The scheme was first established in 1969 in Portage, Wisconsin, in an attempt to provide educational and developmental aid to pre-school handicapped children (Shearer and Shearer, 1972). The Portage technology was imported into the UK in 1976 with a pilot scheme (the Wessex Portage project (Smith *et al.*, 1977)).

It was first introduced to my school in 1979 by a senior member of staff. She supervised a team of five advisers (three teachers and two ancillary helpers). Time was made available for home visits but it was found to be far less time-consuming when parents could come into school for individual training sessions. The supervisor and other team members were always available for support although we did not eventually hold regular group meetings. Parents' workshop meetings were held in school to introduce Portage and, later, as social gatherings for regular Portage users and newer parents who were interested in helping their child.

The scheme has continued in a fairly informal manner for five years and several families have participated. Some of the original children have transferred to other areas or schools and only two of the original advisers have remained at this school. The supervisor has continued the organization and running of the scheme.

The length of time families have continued using Portage has varied considerably from a matter of weeks to as much as three years.

Because of renewed interest in the Portage project from staff members who attended a recent conference and would like to establish a new working team, I felt that it would be of interest to evaluate the present school Portage scheme since its introduction in 1979 and to make recommendations for its future application.

Method of evaluation

A questionnaire and accompanying letter were presented to all parents whose child had participated in the Portage scheme in school since its introduction in 1979.

Several questions were asked concerning details of the scheme:

1 It was most important to know if parents found the scheme helpful either for themselves or for their child (question 8).
2 Completing activity charts is always a worry to parents new to Portage and I wondered how many continued to find this difficult (question 1).

3 I wanted to know if parents would prefer to see 'teachers' in school or in their own homes (question 2).
4 I was most interested in whether pre-school provision would be considered helpful to parents (question 6). (The Portage scheme was first devised and used with pre-school handicapped children.)

Parents' comments were invited in a final section of the questionnaire and, as I hoped that these would be totally unbiased and critical, I promised that all questionnaires would be completely anonymous (question 9).

Sixteen questionnaires were sent out and fifteen were returned completed.

Questionnaire summaries

1 Did you find recording on the activity charts:	easy	5
	fairly easy	9
	quite difficult	1
	difficult	0

We have used a simplified version of the original Portage activity chart as we find that it best suits our aims.

A home teacher in the Wessex Portage project is reported as saying that 'if there were problems with completing charts, it must be the teacher's fault' (Pugh, 1981). I am pleased that only one of our parents encountered any difficulty.

2 Would you prefer to see the Portage adviser/teacher:	in your home	11
	in school	3
	no preference	1

The results of this particular question were most interesting as the majority of our parents and all of those with whom I dealt came into the school.

One parent summed up this preference in her comment, 'professional people, when seen at their place of work, put parents at a disadvantage. You cannot always achieve the best for or from a child if the parent is ill at ease.'

3 Would you prefer to see the Portage adviser/teacher:	weekly	3
	fortnightly	7
	monthly	1
	when necessary	6

Most Portage schemes recommend that parents should be seen on a weekly basis although one, the Portage project in South Glamorgan (Pugh, 1981), is beginning to spread visits over fortnightly or monthly periods in order to extend their help to more families.

Parents in our scheme were initially seen on a weekly basis but this was soon extended to fortnightly visits or in some cases only when necessary (e.g. at the introduction of a new goal or new area of work). This appears to be the most popular choice for our parents (73.3 per cent).

4 How many different tasks would you prefer to work on per week:	one	9
	two	6
	more	0

We have seldom introduced more than one Portage task each week and only when a parent has specifically requested have two been set. The second task has normally consisted of a smaller subsidiary task and has not normally been officially recorded on an activity sheet.

5 Did any other member of your family or friends use the activity charts with your child:	once	1
	occasionally	10
	regularly	2
	never	2

In most instances only the mother was seen with the child and this seems to have influenced the non-participation of other family members. Two fathers are regular visitors with their wives to the school. (I will comment further on this in the evaluation and recommendations section.)

6 Would you have liked to receive the Portage service at home before your child reached school age:	yes	12
	no	2
	n/a	1

Eighty per cent would have liked to receive Portage for their child prior to school age. It is interesting that parents who gave negative comments on the questionnaires would still have liked this service for their child in a pre-school situation and that the parent who felt the question not applicable and who had hardly begun the Portage project expressed a desire to continue Portage. (I considered withdrawing this last questionnaire from the study as the child has not truly completed one Portage task but I found the parent's comments very valuable and have thus included it in all tables and results.)

7 How much time per day did you usually spend on Portage tasks:	15 mins or under	2
	15 to 30 mins	11
	30 to 60 mins	2
	over 60 mins	

The recommended time for Portage tasks in school is 15 to 30 minutes. We feel that longer time is imposing on the child and his or her family. If the task is correctly set by the adviser, and completely understood by the parent, the recommended time need not be exceeded. This is very much a matter of personal choice by the parent but the task should not become an imposition. (I comment further in the next section as this is only a summary.)

8 Did you find the Portage service:

	quite helpful	7
	not at all helpful	2
	very helpful	6

This was a most important question for the Portage scheme we have used during the past five years. I am pleased that 86.7 per cent of our parents have found Portage very helpful or quite helpful.

Both parents who found the scheme 'not at all helpful' made positive comments elsewhere. One parent would be enthusiastic to try Portage again and the other would have liked this service before her child reached school age.

I would have liked to rephrase this question having considered comments received and will comment on this in my 'future recommendations'.

9 Are there any comments you wish to add?

Five parents made no comment on the Portage service. Very favourable comments were made by six parents and negative but helpful comments were made by four parents.

I was very pleased with the response to this small survey with 15 out of 16 questionnaires returned. This surely shows the amount of parental interest and cooperation concerning their child and a positive relationship with their child's school and teachers.

Evaluation and recommendations

In its detailed written curriculum, the stated aims of the school include:

- to broaden the child's horizons through new experiences and new challenges;
- to develop the child's self-esteem through success and achievement;
- to develop independence as far as any disability will allow;
- to involve parents in the care, development and education of their child.

In 1979 it was felt that the introduction of the Portage scheme would help to fulfil these aims and certainly the final one.

The Court Report (1976) comments 'We have found no better way to raise a child than to reinforce the abilities of his parents to do so.'

The need to do something practical to help the child is common to most parents of handicapped children. Parents often feel isolated from their child because they cannot help him or her as they do their other children. They also feel that they should not try what they intuitively think is right, unless an 'expert' has advised it. The result can be non-activity and slower development in the child.

The Warnock Report (1978) points out that children with disabilities or significant difficulties need to be elaborately taught things that other children learn spontaneously and recommends that 'in the earliest years parents rather than teachers should be regarded, whenever possible, as the main educators of their children' (9:1).

The Portage scheme has been criticized as being too dependent on written records and using too large steps between stages. However, it is not intended that the behaviours on the checklist be taken in one large gulp but that teachers should use task analysis and their experience to break down the checklist behaviours so that an individual teaching programme can be developed to suit the needs of particular individuals, taking into account the skills of both parent and child.

The importance of reinforcing success runs right through the Portage project. The only way of achieving success with children whose progress is very slow is to break down each skill to be taught into very small stages.

Since the adviser is working on a one-to-one basis with parent and child, individualization of instructional goals for both is possible. What matters in all approaches is the way in which the checklists are implemented and there are certainly dangers if checklists are used without flexibility and without the addition of further steps as and when they are needed. It is important not to lose sight of the very different needs of individual children and of their parents: the severity of the handicap, the relationships within the family, the living conditions, the number of other children and local community support will all determine the kind of help that a family needs.

Some parents will welcome the intensive involvement of a home-based intervention programme and whilst the structured approach of the Portage projects may provide a life-line for some parents, its very simple structure may be too rigorous for others and may impose considerable strains on families whose ability to cope is already stretched to its limits.

If one is to achieve a true partnership, services must be varied and flexible and based upon the expressed needs of those who use them.

There are varying comments on the questionnaires which aptly illustrate the need for individual programmes.

> I found Portage very helpful, it pointed me in the right direction especially as Andrew was so behind with his 'Milestones'.

> I think that Portage is a very good way of getting a child interested in different kinds of skills.

> We liked doing this Portage as we had the communication with you we felt a part of our child's school work and involved in it.

> I found that certain things that I couldn't get my child to do for me he would do or at least try them with the Portage ... he wanted to have good results at the end.

I think that it is extremely important to choose the right activity at the time the child is showing some interest in the subject otherwise it is a bit tedious at times.

I felt there was too much pressure on me to produce results at regular intervals, therefore I got frustrated with my child.

We have only used Portage for one specific task, this proved unsuccessful.

It is important for the adviser to realize that if projects become a burden they will be counterproductive.

In the United States the most successful programmes were found to be those based in the home with the adviser working regularly in partnership with the mother and involving her directly in activities aimed to foster all aspects of the child's development. A home visit will normally take between 1 and $1\frac{1}{2}$ hours and this time plus travelling cannot normally be spared during a busy school timetable. 73.3 per cent of our parents expressed a preference for seeing the adviser at home and this preference must be considered in future planning. A home visiting schedule would most probably necessitate release from class for the teacher/adviser by another member of staff and, if the whole family is to be involved, some evening visits. This may not be practicable or permissible and must be carefully considered during planning and organization. Portage is a long-term commitment and although an adviser may be prepared to give up some of his or her own leisure time at first, extended evening visiting could become inconvenient and may spoil the atmosphere of the consistent relationship required for success.

The home environment is not only going to play a crucial role in determining the child's behaviour but it is the setting in which most behaviour occurs. There is also the opportunity to involve all members of the family in the teaching process. 'For many handicapped children, and their parents, the experience of succeeding at a specific task and the rewards that this brings cannot start too soon' (Cameron, 1982).

Home visitors tend to see their work as family rather than child centred and are less concerned with the detailed teaching of the skills and completion of charts than with tackling problems which may be affecting relationships within the family. A Portage project for one of my families was specifically a task to keep the child busy after tea so that the mother could tend to a baby brother without the demands of the older child. This was a very successful short-term project which of necessity was completely individual and has not, during the five years, been used for another child.

A programme of self-help skills for another child was abandoned when the parents felt that she would be better employed in academic activities. They worked happily for a number of months during which time the child gained in 3R skills and the parents were pleased with their contribution to her success.

It may be salutary for the home visitor to realize that restricted space, or cold floors, or unhelpful family members, are constant difficulties for the mother as she attempts to work on the programme between visits.

The involvement of other members of the family is a problem which faces school and home visits alike. Most visits take place during the day when the father may be at work and evening or weekend visits are not always practicable either for the family or the adviser.

The dangers of not involving 'family' are self-evident. As the mother's parenting skills and self-confidence increase, so her husband may feel even less involved and able to contribute and although written material is provided for the mother to work from and share with 'others' it is not as effective as a joint programme. Only two of our 'others' worked with their child on a regular basis (see p.8). Other family members can also undo much of the good work undertaken by the mother if they are unfamiliar with the aims and methods in use. It is also important that siblings should not feel neglected when attention is given to the handicapped child on a regular and time-consuming basis.

Although the Wessex Portage project claims that, with carefully structured training, anyone can work successfully with families, some people obviously make better home teachers than others, whether because of their own experience and background or for their ability to relate to the families on the project. The Honeylands Report (Pugh and Russell, 1977) spells out most clearly the considerable amount of tact, patience, sympathy and persistence required for this type of intervention work, and stresses again the need to listen and to reflect the positive side of parents' attitudes. The report emphasizes the importance of willingness to admit failure and to answer questions accountably, and also that the home teacher must not feel the need to dominate the parent. She or he must set a positive aproach for parents who can see no goals or future. Professional skills and knowledge of early child development are highly desirable. The home teacher must be totally reliable and positive and yet take care not to impose unacceptable ideas of child management and development on to the family.

Pringle (1980) comments on 'the extent to which professionals can undermine parents' self confidence in their abilities as parents'. It is apparent that parent and adviser should be compatible if the project is to proceed happily and successfully.

A long-term commitment on the part of professionals providing support is essential. 'To whet the appetite and then withdraw after a few short sessions would surely be irresponsible and counterproductive' (Pugh, 1981). Two questionnaires give evidence of such withdrawal: 'After the Portage chart was returned to school, there was no further contact from the adviser'; 'We were not on the Portage project very long and it just seemed to fade off'. These two questionnaires were among the most negative received and I feel sorry that the parents were disappointed in this way. Consistency is important if the Portage system is to work well and it should be noted that regular completion of activity charts and setting of new tasks can take up much time in a normally busy schedule. I found that occasional failures in Portage tasks were due to my own inconsistency and lack of time in organizing a task rather than to any fault of the parent.

Once an intervention programme has begun and a child has started to make progress, parents may quite understandably develop unrealistic expectations about their child's potential, and may be quite unprepared for, and deflated by, inevitable plateaux when development may appear to stop for a while.

Perhaps, most difficult of all, if parents are to be made to feel responsible for a child's success as he or she acquires new skills, so too will they feel responsible for a child's failures and this can be a very difficult period for all involved, needing tactful and positive handling from the adviser if the parents are not to 'give up'.

A related problem is that of phasing out a particular intervention programme. A regular weekly or fortnightly visit can make a parent too dependent and the gradual phasing out can present problems unless handled sensitively, especially if the parent needs support for a family problem as well as his or her child's learning difficulties.

I regret that I cannot make any assumptions about the success of Portage in increasing the rate of acquisition of tasks or in improving the score in a standard developmental test; I can only comment that there were very few failures in activity tasks during the five years of the scheme and that 86.7 per cent of parents found the service helpful. I would have liked to ask in what way it had been helpful and whether they consider the progress to have been made as a direct result of the scheme. I would also have liked direct comments on their own attitude towards Portage and their child and if they had gained in confidence. In a short survey such as this it was not possible to investigate all possibilities and I would recommend an approach similar to the report of the development and evaluation of the Portage service in South Glamorgan (Revill and Blunden, 1978) which I feel evaluated their Portage project satisfactorily. The Griffiths Mental Development Scale was used on a regular basis with all the children during that particular scheme and gave reliable improvement rates of 13 months over an eight-month period.

My questionnaire results have shown that:

1 93.3 per cent of parents find recording on the activity charts easy or fairly easy.
2 73.3 per cent of parents prefer to see the adviser in their own home – a major problem for the new working team in school.
3 73.3 per cent of parents would like to see the adviser fortnightly or only when necessary – a helpful result which would give the adviser more time to see more parents and which suggests that parents prefer a freer, less demanding routine.
4 All parents express a preference for only one or two tasks per week which I feel is sufficient for the parents of a handicapped child whose

problems in everyday care and management may be very time-consuming without extra tasks.

5 It would be most favourable if both parents could be involved in the Portage tasks but this would necessitate evening or weekend visits. It is pleasing that both parents participated in the tasks occasionally and this may be as much as can be expected in the restricted visiting time available for teachers. Only 13.3 per cent never used the activity charts.

6 80 per cent of our parents would have liked the Portage service at home for their pre-school child (two parents already received it through the educational psychologist) and I feel that this is a definite area of need for all parents of young handicapped children at home. A well-organized Portage scheme or similar type of intervention programme could alleviate the difficulties experienced by many parents and would help to prepare the child better for school and later years. I recommend further investigation into this aspect for all those who are considering the establishment of a Portage advisory team.

7 74.4 per cent of parents spent 15 to 30 minutes each day on Portage tasks with their child. This is adequate and longer periods of time could be counterproductive with parent or child becoming tired or distracted. I have always recommended that the parent should not push any task if the child is unwilling. The activities should be pleasurable and interesting, never a chore, and five minutes of happy work is better than 15 minutes of 'tasks' if they are not enjoyed by child and parent.

8 86.7 per cent of the parents found the service quite helpful or very helpful. This in itself is reason for the continuation of the scheme within school and should provide encouragement for new advisers.

I am satisfied that the Portage scheme has been beneficial in many ways for most of the families involved and hope that my evaluation and recommendations will be useful to those staff members who would like to establish a new working team.

Editors' note: Anne Blake's chapter is an appropriate start to the book, providing a clear introduction to the Portage model,, techniques and materials. Although the Conference was entitled 'Extending and Developing Portage', in the event there was a tremendous need to provide information about Portage at a very basic level. This need was brought about in large part by the availability of money provided by the education support grant to local education authorities.

Foxdenton School has been providing a successful school-based Portage service for many years. Although this scheme is a variation of the traditional model of service delivery it is important to note that the central features that should exist in any scheme have been preserved in this one. Parents are still shown to be central in the development and education of their own children, and the home environment identified as a place where most behaviours will occur. Any concerns about a school-based scheme being bureaucratic, impersonal and excluding parents can be dispelled by this chapter. The sensitivity on the part of the school staff to the needs and activities and individuality of a family as a whole are clearly portrayed and planned for within the context of delivering a Portage service. The author stresses the need to start where parents are at and to provide support that is flexible enough to cater for the individual family needs. This point is nicely illustrated by some quotes from the parents themselves.

Evaluation has been identified in the chapter not only as a check on weekly child progress but also as an aid to making future plans and recommendations about the running of the scheme.

The chapter also emphasizes the features of the Portage adviser's/visitor's role and details skills and personality characteristics which go towards creating a successful partnership with the families.

The reader will readily agree with the final sentiments of the chapter which states satisfaction that the Portage scheme has been beneficial in many ways for most of the families involved.

The Salford Portage in Nurseries Project (SPIN)

Stephanie Lorenz

Introduction

The city of Salford is a small metropolitan authority in Greater Manchester with a school population of around 40,000. Nursery education has always assumed high priority and the city is now served by seven combined nursery centres, eleven nursery schools, three day nurseries and over seventy nursery classes.

While at least six of the authority's twelve special schools cater for children under five there has been an increasing trend for children with special needs to be admitted to mainstream nurseries. This move, while not enshrined in any official local education authority policy, has generally been welcomed by nursery staff. However, it has highlighted the need for better support services and for regular in-service training for nursery personnel.

By the autumn of 1984, a specialist speech therapist had been appointed to work in the nursery centres and to extend the use of the Derbyshire Language Scheme. In addition, physiotherapy and occupational therapy were being provided in nurseries and a central pool of aids and equipment for pre-school children with physical handicaps was introduced.

It was clear that teachers and nursery officers, while keen to work with handicapped children, were lacking both in confidence and in more specialized teaching skills. The psychological service was therefore approached by the nursery adviser and asked to establish a programme of in-service training for staff in the seven separate nursery centres. This created a demand and a follow-up programme for staff in nursery schools was promised, to be followed in due course by training for staff in day nurseries and nursery classes.

Patterns of in-service training

Because the staff were experienced nursery teachers and NNEB trained nursery officers, it was necessary to find a training programme that would supplement and enhance their existing skills rather than replace them. After considering a range of possible formats, it was decided to utilize the

Portage model as a basis for the training programme. The reasons for this decision included the following:

(a) it offers an individual teaching approach to staff normally working in group settings
(b) it provides teaching techniques applicable to the full range of special needs
(c) it embodies basic behavioural principles of value in all teaching
(d) it provides a system of record keeping, enabling progress to be monitored and intervention evaluated.

In setting up a programme of training, the experience of Thomson *et al.* (1978) and Clements *et al.* (1982) were utilized and their model of an introductory workshop, coupled with systematic follow-up and evaluation, adopted. As in their studies, two members of staff from each nursery were invited to participate to:

(a) provide mutual support
(b) ensure the generalization of learned behaviour back into the nursery setting
(c) help the maintenance of Portage activities.

Experiences from the initial Salford workshop suggested that inclusion of the headteacher or matron was advisable as it facilitated the incorporation of Portage programmes into the nursery day as well as providing general support and encouragement. This, therefore, became an integral part of the second and third workshops.

The introductory workshop

Initially, two days were allocated to the basic workshop, with fifteen participants and two main course tutors. However, it was clear that this was not long enough to ensure that course members were sufficiently proficient and confident to cope on their own. Subsequent workshops were, therefore, extended to cover three days.

Since assignments were to be set between sessions, teaching days were spread out over a two week period. Further, as small nursery schools found it hard to release two members of staff at the same time, two parallel courses were run, the second time, allowing staff to be released on alternate days.

The format of the three-day workshop covers the following areas:

(a) observation
(b) defining teaching objectives
(c) use of behavioural language
(d) task analysis

(e) teaching techniques
(f) rewards and punishments
(g) designing a teaching programme
(h) generalization and maintenance
(i) dealing with undesirable behaviours.

While each nursery was provided with checklists and cards from the *Portage Guide to Early Education* (Bluma *et al.*, 1976), these were deliberately introduced towards the end of the workshop. In this way students were forced to develop their own programmes and teaching methods rather than relying on the Portage kit to do it for them.

In addition, students were introduced to a range of checklists and again encouraged to develop their own observation schedules. The Portage checklist itself was found to be of limited value in this context because:

(i) it was considered too detailed for initial screening
(ii) many of the scales overlapped
(iii) expressive and receptive language items were included in the same scale
(iv) fine and gross motor items were included in the same scale
(v) it tended to determine the curriculum, students feeling obliged to work on gaps in the checklist regardless of their importance in real life.

Instead course participants were introduced to a sequential strategy involving the use of:

(a) a problem priority list
(b) a general screening checklist
(c) a detailed checklist, such as Hebden and Whyte (1982) for priority areas.

Much of the course material was derived from Westmacott and Cameron (1981) while back-up was provided by the use of sections of the EDY video (Foxen and McBrien, 1981). Where possible, units using young children were selected to increase their relevance to nursery staff. Those included parts of

Unit 2 : reward assessment
Unit 4 : prompting
Unit 5 : task analysis
Unit 6 : shaping
Unit 7 : imitation

To provide variety, teaching sessions were kept as brief as possible and were interspersed with group work to create an 'active' course (De Sousa,

1985). Role play created a welcome air of levity which hopefully helped students cope with the quantity of work to be covered. Certainly I never realized how many different ways there were to put on a coat!

As the workshop programme indicates, an entire day was set aside for the preparation of a complete teaching programme. Using a standard task analysis sheet and activity chart they produced what one student aptly called a 'knitting pattern' for the teacher.

At the end of the workshop, participants were presented with a loose leaf folder containing copies of overheads, handouts, etc., as well as blank problem priority lists, task analysis and activity chart forms. For as Clayton (1985) comments, course members value some take away material. These then provided a basis for practical work back in the nursery.

Homework assignments

To facilitate the writing of the final teaching programme it was necessary to allow course members to gather relevent information back in their home nursery. Two assignments were therefore set between days 1 and 2 and days 2 and 3.

Assignment 1 concentrated on selection of a target child and general observation, using the problem priority list and screening checklist. Assignment 2 focused on identifying an appropriate teaching target using detailed checklists. Participants were also asked to gather together relevent teaching materials and bring them to the final session. This proved invaluable as assumptions about familiar equipment are all too easily made.

Follow-up (3–4 months)

In setting up the course, nursery heads had been asked to ensure that students were given at least 10 to 15 minutes Portage time per day and this commitment appears to have presented relatively few problems, during the follow-up period at least. Students initially identified a quiet area in which to work, often difficult in a small, open-plan nursery. Office phones were taken off the hook and work carried out in cloakrooms, staffrooms or even Wendy Houses.

Regular Portage times were identified, so that other staff learned not to ask for help at those times and the novelty for the other children soon wore off. Students were asked to work essentially with one child during the follow-up period but when children or students were ill or absent changes were inevitable.

Students in the same nursery were also asked to work together, observing each other's teaching or even swapping children and activity charts to help debug programmes. At monthly intervals, each nursery received a visit from their educational psychologist to iron out problems in situ and comment on their record keeping. In addition, monthly meetings were held for the entire group where experiences could be shared and students helped to realize that everyone else was having the same problems. As one course member remarked: 'It's not as easy as it looks.' Finally, each student was presented with a certificate signed personally by the chief education officer as a 'thank you' for a lot of hard work.

Evaluation

In an attempt to evaluate both the course and the attitude of participants to future Portage activities a questionnaire was distributed at the end of the final group meeting. Combined responses from the first eleven questionnaires indicated that none of the lectures were considered 'not much use', and 70 per cent were 'very useful'. Group meetings were seen as 'very useful' by 73 per cent of course members and 'fairly useful' by the remainder. Frequency and timing were seen as about right by everybody and 91 per cent would be interested in attending further meetings.

Sessions in the nursery were considered 'very useful' by 64 per cent and 'fairly useful' by the rest. Again, frequency and timing were seen as about right with 91 per cent welcoming further sessions.

For the future, 36 per cent thought the training would affect their way of working to a large extent and the remainder to some degree. No one thought it would have no influence. When asked to predict the use over the following six months, 45 per cent thought they would use the various Portage checklists 'frequently' and the remaining 55 per cent occasionally. No one thought they would use them 'rarely'.

When asked for reasons why they might be prevented from using Portage approaches, 82 per cent mentioned shortage of time, 50 per cent organizational problems and 36 per cent lack of suitable children. Nobody considered there to be a lack of support.

Over 90 per cent of course members considered Portage training should be offered to all nursery heads, teachers, matrons and nursery officers. Finally, 82 per cent expressed an interest in more advanced workshops, 82 per cent in using Portage with parents, 64 per cent in helping to train colleagues and 82 per cent in supporting and advising colleagues.

Despite the caution that must be exercised in accepting the validity of questionnaire responses it would appear that the course was well received.

Future activities

Following the success of the first three workshops a fourth is planned for day nursery staff and to fill gaps in other nurseries left by trained staff moving on. Hopefully by the end of 1986 all nursery centres, schools and day nurseries will have a trained head or matron with at least one other trained member of staff and we can move on to the nursery classes.

The Portage bandwaggon, having started to roll, is unwilling to stop. So, in addition, talks are being given to entire nursery staffs and a second tier of Portage tutors and group leaders has been established and used successfully in the second round of workshops.

One nursery head has already written a report on Portage for her governors and the education committee have requested full information on the SPIN project. Finally the interest generated by the scheme so far, coupled with government support, will hopefully allow us to start using Portage with parents.

When I agreed to take on the task of organizing the first workshop I would never have believed that it would have gone so far so fast. However, despite all the hard work, it has certainly been worthwhile and should, in the future, lead to a better deal for all Salford children with special needs.

Editors' note: This chapter clearly illustrates how elements of good practice taken from the Portage model were used to answer the training needs of nursery staff in Salford. Again a development and extension from the original service delivery model but in response to a real need and retaining those elements, such as starting where people are at and recognizing their existing skills and experience and building in a support structure for the individuals concerned.

Stephanie Lorenz also utilizes other models of training such as the Education for the Developmentally Young and the work of Clements et al. to complement her in-service training.

Portage in nurseries is a logical progression from Portage in the home, though the two do not need to be mutually exclusive. What the Salford project does indicate is that flexibility of approach and adaptation of materials may be necessary to suit local needs and personnel. This point was also brought out in the previous chapter by Anne Blake.

Stephanie Lorenz also operationalizes an important aspect of any in-service training, that of follow-up and longer term support after the initial training period. Consistent with behavioural psychology and with maintenance and generalization of skills as outlined in Portage we would expect that for behaviour change to take place and for people to maintain newly acquired skills a supportive structure over time should be made available to them.

Like Portage itself this extension and development in Salford appears to be going from strength to strength and provides valuable information to those of us who are both active in in-service work and in using Portage in a variety of contexts.

A Task Analysis of Setting up a Portage Scheme

Maria Evans and Anna Wright

A pilot study was initiated in the Spelthorne district of north-east Surrey in October 1983 to determine whether Portage could meet local needs. The initiative came from two educational psychologists working in the area who had a particular interest in working with children with severe and complex learning difficulties and their parents. Both also visited local special schools for children with severe learning difficulties on a time contracted fortnightly basis.

Using Portage practice we present a task analysis of setting up and funding a Portage scheme, with very little financial back-up.

Objective: the educational psychologists to set up and arrange funding for a Portage scheme for ten families in the Spelthorne area of Surrey by April 1986.

Task analysis

1 Attend Portage training course.
2 Discuss with area education officer, principal educational psychologist and inspector for special education suitable model of Portage delivery for the target area.
3 Send letter inviting senior staff in all relevent services in the area asking them to attend meeting to discuss the possibility of setting up a multi-disciplinary management team to oversee a pilot project.
4 Hold meeting outlining plan for Spelthorne Portage project.
5 Send out detailed plan of the scheme to all who attended the management team meeting with further information on Portage.
6 Hold second meeting and arrange dates for the first Portage training course. Management team members submit names of professionals wishing to attend and children they consider might benefit from Portage.
7 Consultant paediatrician discusses Portage with parents of pre-school children.
8 Order Portage materials.

9 Run three-day Portage training course. At end of course ask for people interested in doing Portage visiting and attending weekly supervision sessions.
10 Hold first staff meeting and match visitors to families.
11 Write to parents telling them who their home visitor is.
12 Commence weekly visits and supervision sessions.
13 Hold three-monthly management team meetings.
14 Project evaluated after six months.
15 Collate results and apply for joint funding.

Detailed explanations of each step, and a description of the scheme including difficulties encountered and overcome are given below.

Step 1: Obtain Portage training

The psychologists were Portage trained – one by way of EDY (at the Hester Adrian Centre), running parent workshops and attending a Portage course run by R.J. Cameron for interested members of the LEA, the other through recent training at University College London including Portage as part of the course. Surrey teachers had shown an interest in Portage, workshops using Portage materials had been run so that all the staff in the local special school were aware of Portage and many were using the techniques as part of daily classroom practice.

Step 2: Discussion with other professionals

We discussed our ideas with colleagues in the education service and received interest and support from our county educational psychologist, area education officer and inspector for special education. All reminded us that they could provide little or no funding and that what we did must be done within our staffing limits.

Discussion with the area school psychological service team about the extra workload implied by a Portage commitment encouraged us to continue despite this and undertake a pilot scheme with regular Portage training workshops. These would be made available to all those interested even if they were not going to be home teachers, since we believed that the more actively involved people were, the less threatened they were likely to be by what was happening in their families. Experience has made us aware that professional conflict can occur when people working with the same families do not know what others are doing.

Initially, other professionals working in the field were not always as enthusiastic or convinced as we were but it seemed worth exploring the matter further.

Step 3: First letter

Following the Winchester Portage model, we established a management team by sending a letter inviting representatives of education, health and social services to an initial meeting at the education office. It must be added at this point that relationships between the disciplines were very good and had been developed over a number of years.

Step 4: First management team meeting

The response to the letter inviting them to the meeting was good and all agencies were represented. We discussed Portage, outlined plans and asked for comments and their support as a management team.

Step 5: Initial plan

Following this meeting, we sent out a detailed plan of the scheme to all who attended together with further information on Portage – articles, etc. – which we had read and found useful. This proved to allay some of the team members' fears relating to:

- the creation of unrealistic parental expectations
- putting pressure on children rather than respecting their limitations
- whether home visitors could be trained as effective teachers
- whether parents could teach their own children.

We were able, with the help of the literature, to convince them that Portage represents a highly effective technology which allows parents to teach children with special educational needs important new skills.

The Portage management team that we had at this stage consisted of:

area educational psychologist – in the chair
educational psychologist – secretary to the team
deputy area education officer – education representative (admin.)
inspector for special education
social work team leader
senior clinical medical officer
medical officer for special school (SLD)
consultant paediatrician
senior nurse manager
senior nurse child health

Only at a later date did we coopt a GP representative and are now considering the addition of a parent representative.

Step 6: The second management team meeting

At the second management team meeting we had arranged that members would bring with them the names of anyone who wished to attend the first Portage training workshop. We would later write to thank those interested, and provide them with details of the course contents, dates and venue.

We also asked for the names of children whose families might benefit from the Portage scheme. We decided to run a pilot scheme for six children for six months, evaluate the effects and then make a formal application for funding. Choosing six children from the list proved to be a problem but we finally chose the six youngest and excluded children attending full-time education. To evaluate the scheme, the school medical officer would assess the children using the Griffiths Mental Development Scales before and after Portage visiting started. The educational psychologists would record the number of new skills learned and devise a parental questionnaire.

Step 7: Informing the parents

The consultant paediatrician would discuss Portage with these families and ask them if they would like to join the scheme. Subsequent new referrals would be addressed to the chairperson and discussed with the management team.

Step 8: Obtaining Portage materials

Money reared its head at this point as we only had two Portage sets and felt six more would be needed. The educational psychologists were given the task of finding funding for these – education agreed to buy them for us.

Step 9: The workshop

Those attending the first course included speech and physiotherapists, school medical officer, senior nurse manager, health visitors, social worker, headteacher, class teacher, playgroup teacher, and community psychiatric nurse (15 people in all).

The workshop was run over three days and divided into sessions which were strictly adhered to in terms of both time and content. It was felt to be important:

(a) that the course was skills based
(b) that a fluency level of skill should be established
(c) that there should be active participation whenever possible.

To do this we used the following techniques:

1 Frequent repetition to produce overlearning.
2 Modelling – providing examples of all techniques before practice.
3 Breaking tasks into small components and teaching them in steps.
4 Providing self-checking systems to help check that all components of a task are remembered.
5 Participation by course members to produce examples first in groups, then in pairs, then individually.
6 Positive feedback after each example. Participants are not allowed to fail – failure belongs to us because we have not taught well enough.
7 Showing the objectives of each session to the group. They can judge for themselves at the end of each session whether or not we have met our objectives (thus seeing Portage techniques in practice).
8 Role play to test generalization of the skills.
9 Video material to:

   – put skills into context
   – prove that it works
   – provide examples
   – use for practical work (e.g. recording a baseline).

10 Frequent planned reference to personal experience of course tutors (e.g. of Portage home visiting).

The first two days of the workshop had set homework which was discussed by the whole group the following morning. Although the timing was tight, we encouraged active participation and interaction from the group members at all times.

We have run this course three times now and on each occasion the participants have been lively, have obviously enjoyed it (and so have we), and have acquired the skills we aimed to teach them. Follow-up observation of the teachers on the course indicates that they use the skills taught to good effect and that they find it much easier than before to devise and carry out individual programmes. Liaison with parents has also improved.

At the end of the first workshop, we asked for volunteer home visitors who were prepared to take on Portage for at least six months as part of their existing workload (this arrangement had been previously agreed with senior staff.) Seven people put their names forward. The group consisted of health visitors, speech and physiotherapists, a social worker and a teacher (who later had to drop out because of unforeseen staffing difficulties in school). We arranged to contact them by post within the next couple of weeks to set the date of the first supervision meeting. Setting the times of supervision meetings with so many busy professionals proved a problem but this was not insurmountable. Thursday afternoon between 3.00 and 4.00 proved to be the best fit. It was made clear at the outset that regular attendance at the supervision meeting was part of the home visitors' contract with us. Real Portage training occurs continuously in the context of discussion and problem solving at these weekly meetings.

Step 10: Which visitor? Which family?

Two weeks later, we began our first meeting at the local child guidance clinic. Where possible we arranged for home teachers to visit families that were already on their caseload or where travel was cut to the minimum (bearing in mind lack of funding).

The home visitors were armed with their equipment: Portage cards, activity charts, books for parents and lots of enthusiasm. The format of the supervision meeting was discussed and the importance of regular attendance was stressed.

Step 11: Letter to parents

We then wrote to the parents letting them know the name of their home visitor and that they would be getting in contact shortly.

Step 12: Running staff meetings

The meetings follow a set pattern beginning with a cup of tea. Each visitor in turn then describes the result of the last task left with the parents, the next task set and outlines any difficulties experienced with recording, setting tasks or general problems encountered. The supervisors keep blank activity charts, record sheets, toys to lend to families, and arrange home visits to set six-monthly goals.

The supervision sessions have been an interesting learning experience. Benefits accrue to everyone when a group of committed professionals can work together on common and shared specific problems. Each professional contributes as a practising home teacher rather than as an external consultant to the service and each brings different expertise which provides a regular flow of ideas concerning new ways to approach tasks.

Some of the problems encountered were certainly more than we as supervisors had bargained for as, most sadly, one of the children died during our initial six months. This had, quite understandably, a devastating effect on the home teacher who had been working with the family. The whole group acted as a support in this situation. Some of the more typical problems are described below:

> Carol, who suffers from cerebral palsy, was unable to do very much at initial visit but the home visitor quickly discovered that this was because she did not have a suitable chair to sit in. She subsequently learned the highest number of skills in the first six months.
>
> Sam has Down's syndrome and is now at a mainstream nursery. Initially his mother abandoned the charts in the middle of each week, and the

> younger child could not be persuaded to leave her lap. Sam learned to read eight words in three months.
>
> Danny has Down's syndrome and refused to sit in his chair for more than a few seconds on first visits. After a few weeks he was in his chair waiting at his table before the home visitor had rung the doorbell.

Successes are shared by all. The supervision sessions are vital. They provide a relaxed forum for discussion and advice. Visitors can be encouraged and reminded of the importance of charting and writing attainable goals. However, it is a time-consuming activity in a service which is already under pressure. We, in turn, have been encouraged by our colleagues and by the feedback we have had on Portage.

Step 13: Running management team meetings

The management team meets regularly every three months. At each meeting, a brief resumé is given of the progress made by the children, new referrals are brought forward and discussed, future training courses planned, charities approached for toys and pictures to be used on home visits and submission for funding discussed. Each meeting held has been positive and supportive. The team meetings allow discussion on each child's progress and facilitate links between the services.

Step 14: Evaluation

The effects of the scheme were evaluated in three ways:

(a) By Griffiths assessments before and after Portage visiting had begun
(b) By parental questionnaire
(c) By totalling the number of skills learned.

Although the project was originally planned for six children incomplete results are available because one child died, another started full-time education and one home visitor became ill during the first six months. When a child left the scheme another was introduced.

Griffiths test results
As Griffiths assessments were already available on some of the children, it was not possible to arrange for the tests to be carried out at precisely the beginning and the end of the project.

Name	Griffiths Quotient 1st test	2nd test	Time between testing	Change in GQ
Carol	91%	97%	7 mths	+6%
Jane	51%	49%	9 mths	−2%
Celia	39%	35%	1 yr 1 mth	−4%
Danny	66%	62%	1 yr 4 mths	−4%
Sam	77%	77%	1 yr 7 mths	no change

As it was not possible to have a control group, these results do not provide useful information. Except in the case of Carol, the changes in the scores did not exceed the standard error on the test. We realized, belatedly, that it may not have been totally appropriate to use a test that aims to measure unchanging mental abilities to assess the effectiveness of a scheme that aims to teach new skills.

Parental questionnaire (7 parents)
The parental questionnaire produced a very positive response. All the parents replied that they would recommend the service to others, that the charts were easy to use, that they got on well with the home visitor, and all those who received an uninterrupted service felt their child's progress was better than usual. They also commented that they looked forward to the home visits, found them helpful and wished they could have received the service earlier. The following are examples of the comments received:

> I have felt that I have got tremendous support and cannot praise this scheme enough.

> I found it very helpful in guiding my teaching as Sam was my first child, and I had no idea what a normal child his age should know.

> My daughter Linda was only on the scheme a few weeks, but I found it very useful as there were aims to achieve and helpful advice on how to set about achieving them.

> I wish I had been able to participate in the scheme before Celia had started school, when I had more time to sit and feel despondent at her lack of progress and my apparent inability to help her learn new skills.

> Advantages: we found we were more likely to do the activities with Jane when we had a chart to fill in. Also Jane benefited from repeating the same procedures several times. Disadvantages: None.

Skills learned

The number of skills learned in each area of the checklist are presented below.

Name	Months visited	Motor	Social	No. of skills learned Lang.	Cogn.	Self Help	Total
Celia	6	10	4	6	3	3	26
Jane	6	8	10	4	7	2	31
Danny	4	6	3	0	6	8	23
Carol	4	12	12	20	16	7	69
Zoe	2	1	0	2	6	4	13
Linda	1	0	0	1	3	0	4
Sam	6	5	9	12	9	12	47

These results indicate that the children learned an average of seven new skills a month. This rate of gain is similar to that reported in the Wessex Portage project evaluation (Pugh, 1981).

Step 15: Funding

At the start of the project the source of funding favoured was joint finance from the health and education authorities. We were concerned to preserve the multi-disciplinary nature of the home teaching team and for this reason we did not favour an application for one or two Portage workers. Instead we submitted an application for 25 hours per week of home teaching time to be split between the different services as follows:

No. of hours per week	Professional who would visit	Approx annual cost
5	Speech therapist	£1161
5	Physiotherapist	£ 949
5	Social worker	£1040
5	Health visitor	£1084
5	Teacher	£1372

In addition to this we requested one session ($3\frac{1}{2}$ hours) per week of educational psychologist's time, one hour per week of clerical officer's time and £1000 for equipment. This would enable us to deliver a Portage service to ten families. The total sum requested over three years is just over £23,000. The response initially has been favourable but no money is available until after April 1986. We are now revising our proposal for submission to the DES through the education authority. Unfortunately, the structure laid down by the DES makes provision for the appointment of full-time Portage workers and does not fit the structure for which we have applied. We are continuing the scheme using volunteers and are currently awaiting a response to our applications.

Conclusion

In this scheme we have aimed to:

(a) teach pre-school children new skills;
(b) teach parents a set of techniques which they can use successfully with their children well into the future;
(c) provide useful ongoing support to parents at a much needed time by allowing regular discussion of problems as they arise;
(d) provide a forum for interdisciplinary communication and sharing of expertise in relation to the pre-school child;
(e) provide a basis for the formal assessment under the 1981 Education Act;
(f) improve the skills of professionals working with handicapped children in the Spelthorne area.

We feel that we have achieved our aims but are being made increasingly aware that parents of handicapped youngsters in other parts of our authority also want Portage. We are encouraging and training other colleagues in the Surrey school psychological service in the hope that in the future Portage will be available to all parents who want it.

Editors' note: This chapter provides a very detailed and sequential account of how one might go about setting up a Portage project in an area where no additional resources, at least in the short term, are going to be forthcoming. It emphasizes the merits of a multi-disciplinary approach to meeting the needs of children with severe learning difficulties both at management team level and the home visitor level. Cooperation is a key note throughout the fifteen stages of the setting-up of the project with a clear indication of the various roles.

This project highlights many of the financial problems which have bedevilled Portage projects up and down the country, but the enthusiastic and systematic approach of the authors shows what can be done even on a shoestring. Hopefully the provision of the education support grant will reward projects such as this and others who have also been modelling good practice against the odds. When money is available, other areas of the country will be able to use these task analysed experiences of the authors to set up their own successful projects.

The chapter itself started with a question about whether Portage could be used to meet the local needs of the district in north-east Surrey. We are able to see quite clearly that the answer is an emphatic 'yes' to this question and that demands are also being made to service other districts of the county.

Portage in Bradford: Training Volunteers

Paul Wiehl and Patsy Barrow

Introduction

Following difficulties in obtaining appropriate funding the Bradford and Keighley Pilot Portage made a successful bid to the community programme funding. A large proportion of this money was then used to provide information to groups and to train volunteers from the community and provide expenses for them.

Background to the scheme

Bradford is a large metropolitan authority covering an area of 37,010 hectares with a total population of 464,000. It has a 0-19 population of 143,400. A total of 106,800 are school age and there are 36,600 children under the age of five.

At one end of Bradford metropolitan district is Keighley and it was here in October 1982 that a group comprising Dr Barnardo's workers, a psychologist and two social workers, began a small pilot scheme based on Portage guidelines.

In November 1982 a small group of specialist health visitors, two psychologists and three peripatetic teachers also began a pilot scheme at the Bradford City end of the authority. Two pilot schemes therefore were in operation and in April 1983 they were evaluated.

The evaluation exercises consisted of collecting data on tasks and collecting the comments of home visitors and parents.

Pilot studies

In the pilot study (Bradford) seven home visitors completed questionnaires and six of them offered full breakdowns of each task set, including dates and the criteria used for success.

Seven parents also completed an initial questionnaire before or during the early phase of their involvement with the scheme.

Four of the parents completed a questionnaire at a later point in the scheme. All four indicated that the scheme had been helpful. All of the visitors also expressed their support for the scheme in their questionnaires.

One of the concluding comments in the evaluation reads:

> As can be seen from both the parents' and the home visitors' statements the pilot scheme was successful as an evaluation exercise. If one takes as a representative sample the information presented by six of the home tutors one can see the success. (Of the 86 tasks set, 80 per cent were completed successfully (70/86).) One should also note that seven of the tasks set were not completed because of illness factors.

In the pilot study (Keighley), responses to a questionnaire to parents (nine) had indicated that eight had found it helpful and one had found it both helpful and unhelpful in certain aspects.

The other responses are listed below:

1 Have you found the scheme .....
Helpful (8) Unhelpful (10) Both (1)

2 If helpful, in what ways?
Regular home visits (1)
Concentrating on one particular task (1)
Understanding what the child is capable of achieving (2)
Suggestions for play materials and activities (2)
Working to a teaching schedule with definite goals (4)
Increasing the child's attainments (2)
Increasing awareness of developmental stages (2)
Awareness of progress (1)
Providing a natural focus and coordination point for supportive professionals (1)
Contact with others, decreasing isolation (1)

3 If unhelpful, how?
Inappropriate tasks causing child to become frustrated (1)

4 What other benefits (if any) have resulted from your participation in the scheme?
Made more aware of the child's abilities in the wider sense (2)
Opportunity to discuss problems of handicap in general (2)
The fact that the child made demonstrable progress proved personally encouraging (1)
Parent felt more competent (1)
Access to factual material from the home adviser (1)
Greater awareness of the best ways to teach handicapped children (1)
Providing a good basis on which to liaise with school (1)

The Bradford pilot document also contained comments supporting an 'expansion' of the scheme and on 9th June 1983 the evaluations were presented to Bradford representatives from health, education and social services. Though the evaluations were received with enthusiasm, there was much less enthusiasm for any jointly or otherwise funded approach to expand the schemes at that time.

This was particularly unfortunate as the team were very short of equipment and also the specialist health visitors working on the scheme were due to drop out as their workload was too large. The Bradford district nursing officer could unfortunately offer us no solace in this matter.

Obtaining funding

The Keighley project could continue and build on its initial pilot success due to the involvement and coordination of Dr Barnardo's workers, while the Bradford project was in danger of sinking quietly into the past, with only an evaluation document to show for its success. Therefore in order to expand there was a need to look elsewhere for funding. One of the authors attended several meetings of the Forum for Young Families, a collection of community groups and projects for the under-fives. Many were funded by the community programme fund (previously called urban aid) and the basic tenents of Portage fitted well with the description of the priorities for schemes likely to be able to obtain such funding. In Bradford a section of community programme money is reserved especially for the under-fives though the amount available does fluctuate.

In due course a bid was formulated and submitted for consideration. During the same period a bid was also formulated to the EEC Mis-à-Niveau scheme, a European Community training fund, and unfortunately this bid was rejected because it did not fulfil the necessary criteria. However the community programme money was forthcoming (£14,000 divided over three years into £8,000, £3,000, £3,000). Our first amount (£8,000) arrived in September 1984 for the financial year 1984/85. This time delay effectively reduced our first financial year to six months, though we were allowed to carry over the remaining capital, though not the revenues into the next year (Table 1).

Table 1: Community programme

Community Programme Award £14,000	Capital	Revenues
Year 1 (1984/85)	£5,000	£3,000
Year 2 (1985/86)		£3,000
Year 3 (1986/87)		£3,000
Total	£5,000	£9,000 = £14,000

The money has now been used to buy materials and equipment needed, and also fund the advertising, organization, planning and running of a number of introductory days and the subsequent training course days.

Training course

Introductory days

These days consisted of information, videos, discussions and exercises presented in a relatively informal manner. The main elements are:

1 Introduction to Portage
2 Behavioural language
3 Getting information about a problem
4 The Portage process
5 Using the materials
6 Information about the schemes operating
7 Pros, cons and adaptations
8 Feedback/plenary

The days were attended by a wide variety of people most of whom work directly with children under five.

Training days

In February 1985 an opportunity was offered to all who had attended the introductory days to participate in a longer training course to be run during March and April 1985. Nineteen people applied with two subsequently dropping out before the start of the course. The course consisted of seven sessions run on Tuesdays and Thursdays over one month in the Peace Studies department, Bradford University. The hours of the course were 10.00 a.m. to 2.30 p.m. including lunch to ensure that parents of school age children could participate easily; a crèche was organized for the younger children. This meant that there was a course length of 24 hours, and with the introductory day each trainee had nearly 30 hours' tuition.

Course elements

In planning the content and follow-up to the course we took account of Brian Daly's guidelines for workshops and of many other Portage workshops. We also received correspondence from people we contacted including a valuable course outline and letter from Clare Jones, psychologist, from Gwent, who wrote that in her view 'most professions need at least a week's course and then intensive supervision for a year'. Providing one extends the term 'profession' to include parents, we found this a most useful concept in encouraging us to adopt a personal supervision system as well as the supervision group, for all new Portage home visitors.

The course itself consisted of the following elements. Video material was used throughout the course for information, exercises and for getting points across in a humourous way:

1 Portage materials, techniques and principles:
This included practice from video on checklist and charting, elements from behavioural psychology (prompting objectives task analysis, rewards, etc.) and mirrors much that is being presented in most workshops around the country, if our research is correct.

2 Other professionals and referral routes:
We used parents (some having children with special needs) to look at numbers of professionals involved and any other established order in which this involvement occurred. This was supplemented from our own lists and from information from video, and guest speakers on the roles of the two child development centres in Bradford and Keighley. Most early referrals to Portage had arrived through these two centres though increasingly other routes are being developed.

This led to an expansion of knowledge for everyone, including the tutors, of what pressures may occur for a family who have a child who is diagnosed 'developmentally slow' by the medical profession. The large number of professionals who may be involved at this stage and over the next few months and years can be very confusing to parents. This tended to confirm our decision to include in the seminars on Portage process, the role of a good, friendly listener and a possible 'clarifier' to the family.

The session also provided information on the routes that Portage referrals may take in our area:

(i) Direct from professional (e.g. senior medical officer, paediatrician, health visitor, psychologist);
(ii) Child development centres (professional joint referrals or through members of the Portage supervision groups who work at the centres);
(iii) Parents (an increasing trend);
(iv) Other agencies including education, social services, pre-five and community groups.

3 Supervision:
The personnel and structure of Portage were outlined to participants, including the role of supervision groups. The proposal of personal supervisors for these participants who wished to become home visitors with the scheme, was introduced. The participants also had the opportunity of meeting many of the supervisor's group members and all of the personal supervisors.

4 Play:
There have been some criticisms on the lines of 'Portage as a recipe book' rather than part of a family attitude approach and system. We were keen to include reference to 'play' in all the course but also decided to create a 'play section' using Roy McConkey's 'Let's Play' video course as a basis. As readers will be aware, the creation of any 'sections' in any approach, course, conference or manifesto creates both supporting and opposing feeling and this proved to be no exception. It is thought likely that we will seriously review this element before our next course.

5 Working with ethnic minorities:
The issue of working with families from the ethnic minorities was raised constantly throughout the course, supplemented by video examples of home visiting to black families. Having two black participants, who subsequently became home visitors, also helped us to keep these issues in focus throughout the course. The team still feel that this issue needs further attention from all Portage schemes, and that materials are still urgently in need of some translation.

6 'Working with families':
Our main aim in this part of the training programme was to move away from the techniques of teaching skills to expose the tensions, anxieties and enjoyment of working with families on the Portage scheme.

During our preparation for the course we drew on the skills of fellow professionals in the psychological service who were involved in family work of various kinds. We were anxious to present a realistic picture of the problem which can arise from the developing relationship between the Portage worker and the family and the stages in the process. However, we were also aware of the dangers of overwhelming our volunteers with theories which led them to feel like ill-equipped counsellors rather than Portage home visitors.

We decided on four major themes and these are outlined below:

(i) *Exploring individuals' reaction to handicap*
We felt that we needed to acknowledge and give time to express our feelings about 'handicap' to allow people to express fears, anxieties or even revulsion in an atmosphere of acceptance. We hoped that this would mirror the support volunteers would receive in the future within the supervision group.

Two films shown in the seminar were presented to provide a catalyst for discussion. The first film showed a physiotherapist working with a profoundly multiply handicapped child. The second was a film of Dick Boydell and Jane Abler, two adults with cerebral palsy trying to communicate with each other through a helper (BBC, *Horizon*).

After the films the volunteers broke up into small groups for discussions. Many issues were raised in these discussions. We found we had underestimated the need for volunteers to share their experiences and had perhaps failed to be aware of how close and supportive the group had become. Many of the course members felt able to share painful memories and grief. It was a salutary lesson to hear people recall distress inflicted by 'professionals' by an ill-timed remark or patronizing manner.

(ii) *Counselling skills*

Portage home visitors, often by virtue of their consistency in visiting families, can often be seen as key workers. We need to be aware of the problems involved with the family while accepting that some visitors are frequently in the 'front line'. They can face intense feelings of anger and despondency as well as sharing the joy and elation when a child achieves a task. Listening to parents is a vital skill. Many parents complain of their wishes not being heard. Portage hinges on a partnership with parents and listening to their views is a vital component. Skill in listening may also help other problem areas to be acknowledged and the Portage visitor can help by providing information about where to go with financial problems or for medical advice, etc.

In our course we included a morning session incorporating interviewing techniques and skills developed on a counselling course run by the School and Family Service. Exercises included working in small groups of three with two participants and an observer. We worked at non-verbal communications and at role playing in different situations – reversing roles to give the participants an opportunity to describe how the experience had felt.

Some intrepid souls even braved being videoed in an interview.

(iii) *The process of change*

We wanted to look at Portage as a basic tool rather than a rigid recipe, with a family's needs determining how it is used. An attempt was made to look at Portage in a variety of family settings. From this followed the idea of families as dynamic and changing. Portage is itself a tool of change.

The process of change by which Portage becomes an intrinsic part of the process of educating the young child is one that is difficult to 'map out'. However, one model, developed by Speck and Attneave (1973) looked at family network processes in relation to other agencies. They proposed a model that we found helpful to outline in the course.

This model of change has seven stages:

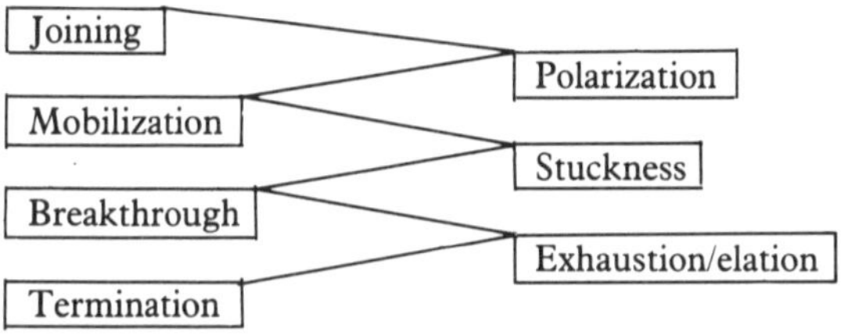

This model, like all models, will not fit every case or experience. However, each stage may strike recognizable notes in many workers.

Joining: Early introduction to Portage involves the parent and home visitor coming together in a spirit of desired partnership. Pleasantries are also exchanged and a rapport is developed.

Polarization: The home visitor and the parent at this point need to state explicitly their role and the extent of their involvement. Effectively it means standing back and saying what each has to offer. A contract of a sort is formed.

Mobilization: Early efforts put into initial tasks can set the programme off to a good start and occasionally this phase continues.

Stuckness: However, the programme after its initial novelty can lead both participants into a 'stuckness' or phase when either disillusionment sets in or either the visitor or parent, or both, feel they are getting nowhere and excuses may arise. At this point it is difficult to avoid returning to a joining or polarization phase where Portage may be discredited or blamed in some manner.

Breakthrough: Sticking to the tasks in hand will eventually lead to a breakthrough and a clear partnership, even though this could just be an agreement that the steps for a task were wrong.

Exhaustion/elation: The end of a task, activity or programme should be accompanied by acknowledging the achievement and congratulating each other on the planning, organization and completion of the task.

Termination: The choice to move on to another step, task or programme or to close Portage for the present is made at this point. If further work is to be done the process repeats itself as the partners join for the 'next dance'.

(iv) *Resistances*
Finally, we had a light-hearted brainstorm session about ways for preventing Portage getting into the 'stuckness' stage. This was considered from both the viewpoint of the family and the home visitors. Some of the home visitors present at this session revealed their hidden ploys! We all identified with the feeling of relief after a timid knock at the door and a hasty retreat to the car. Who hasn't forgotten their charts or been a little rushed? In the seminar we asked people to join us in the exercise, a two-minute brainstorm on how we avoid tasks, trying to be as clear and honest as possible.

Course outcomes

Of the 17 people on the course six people wished to become home visitors immediately; four of these were parent volunteers, the other two were a social worker with the School and Family Service (formerly the School Psychological Service) and a worker with the Spastics Society and Family Service Unit. Three more parent volunteers hoped to start at a later date depending on their domestic circumstances.

Two nursery nurses from a social service day nursery requested further support for their work in the nursery and are supported in working with the Portage materials and making occasional home visits; regular visits by members of the Portage team are made to the nursery. The nursery has already indicated its desire to send other staff on future courses.

The two social service family aides on the course hoped to include Portage work in their brief, and both expressed an interest in becoming part of the team in the future. A speech therapist on the course offered supervision support and advice where necessary.

A parent from outside Bradford was helped in making contact with a psychologist in her area who hopes to work with her on the curriculum needs of a special school using Portage. Two volunteers decided not to pursue any further involvement with Portage at that stage.

The continued outcomes of the introductory/information days has led to the position whereby a number of playgroups, nurseries and special schools have their own materials and a regular visit by a member of the Portage team who monitors and discusses the adaptation of the Portage principles and techniques into their working environment. This we feel, offers a much more sustained and relevant approach than using workshop only approaches.

Implementing the scheme

Since the pilot study evaluations the team has concentrated on using the funding as well as is possible for a team without any appointed Portage administrator. This situation may change if the Bradford education support grant for additional team(s) is successful.

The project is currently in the following position:

1 There is a single management team/committee comprising a selection of the following: psychologists, social workers, advisers, senior medical officer, Dr Barnardo's project coordinator, speech therapists, peripatetic teacher, voluntary bodies' representatives. It has recently been agreed to add representation from the parent volunteers working on the scheme to the list. This group meets on a six-weekly basis on average.

2 There are two supervisor groups, one operating in Bradford, the other in Keighley. Dr Barnardo's continue to coordinate the supervision group in Keighley. A recent meeting of the management team produced recommendations on the way that both groups should develop by incorporating aspects of each other's procedures and format. The Keighley group meet on a fortnightly basis. The Bradford group met on a weekly basis for the three months following the course before agreeing to adopt a fortnightly format.

3 There are 14 home visitors, statutory and voluntary workers combined. The statutory workers (ten) are allowed by their directorate to do Portage. The voluntary workers receive expenses for travel, childminding, materials and attendance at courses and conferences including the National Conference and also the full insurance cover of the local education authority.

The 14 home visitors comprise the six from the course, one of whom works in both Bradford and Keighley areas. The eight other home visitors are the remainder of those who participated in the original pilot studies, comprising two social workers, four peripatetic teachers, a Barnardo's worker and a psychologist.

4 Currently a total of 35 families receive Portage home visiting and a large number of other children receive some adapted form of Portage in a pre-five setting.

Personal supervision

Each new Portage home visitor is paired with a current visitor, one of the eight experienced visitors mentioned above, who is available for contact at all times and is also present at the supervision group meetings. Initially the volunteer will accompany the personal supervisor.

Once a new family has been contacted and 'customership' confirmed (e.g. by a short visit by the coordinator to the scheme or by the personal supervisor) a first joint visit is made by the supervisor and new home visitor. The aim here is for a 'contract' to be set up between the family and the visitor. A second joint visit may follow, to continue to establish the Portage procedure as necessary. Following this the personal supervisor meets the visitor on a regular basis to discuss the progress and may carry out joint visits occasionally or in liaison with involved professionals. The guidelines for the personal supervision obviously vary with the needs of each family but in general the aim is for the supervisor to adopt a 'backseat' role as quickly as possible and to encourage a working relationship between the home visitor, parent(s) and child.

Open records are kept by the supervisor on his/her contacts with the home visitor in a Proposal Action Outcome form and initially joint reports are made to the supervisor group by the personal supervisor and visitor.

During the Conference presentation the question of placing responsibility on volunteer home visitors was raised. We were fortunate to have two of the volunteers present who commented on this aspect, citing the personal supervisor's arrangement as the major significant factor in reducing any feelings of isolation and/or the pressure of responsibility.

Evaluation studies

1 Since the initial pilot studies there has been one interim evaluation study, in the Keighley area, which has revealed the continuation of the success rate of tasks predicted in the pilot study.

2 Following the course feedback sessions in which comments were collected and scrutinized, a questionnaire was sent to all course participants. Early returns were analysed; the trend would appear to be very favourable, though some of the negative comments collected at the end of the course also appear again. These are being taken into account in the planning of the next course.

3 Contact with the diverse population using some form of Portage or with each individual who attended a day course is being discussed in light of the need for further evaluation compared with the time required for such an undertaking.

4 Parents' comments on Portage are also being collected for evaluation and possible inclusion in a new Portage booklet being designed and produced by an Upper School Learning Resource department, funded by the programme.

5 Personal supervisor's evaluation of new home visitor's success rates suggest that following occasional minor initial problems tasks are being completed to the level predicted by the pilot study.

6 A further fuller evaluation of the Bradford and Keighley Portage is planned to take place in the future in order that it could support a further bid to community programmes if necessary, when the current money runs out in March 1987.

Seminar discussion

During the seminar the following general points were raised by the presenters and commented on by the audience, regarding the use of community money and the training of parent volunteers in Bradford.

The pros

1 We feel we have used community money to offer information and training to individuals and groups, voluntary and statutory in the community.
2 We believe that process of training further erodes the false dichotomy of expert/non-expert client roles so often prevalent in under-five work.
3 We feel that Portage offers both skills and greater confidence to the parents and groups in the community, in order for them individually and collectively to have more of a say in their future and in the future of their children.

The cons

1 We fear that having volunteers in the scheme could be criticized as cheap labour, or even used that way by unscrupulous people/authorities.
2 Anxiety may be raised on both sides as parent volunteers may experience some resistance by professionals to accept them as co-workers. This issue was seen to have been partly answered previously by the parent volunteers' comments on personal supervision.
3 There is a further wider issue to the involvement of Portage in the under-five sector. In Bradford we are catering for less than 40 per cent of all three- and four-year-old children in terms of nursery education. In the light of the 1981 Education Act, which recognizes the needs of pre-five children more and requires children with special needs to have greater opportunity to enter mainstream education, there is a need to increase the overall provision so that waiting lists are reduced and so that integration can take place in the right proportions, i.e. so that we do not overload our small mainstream sector with unbalanced or skewed populations of children with special needs and/or create hostility in local parents whose child may still be on a waiting list.

We also continue to believe in increasing knowledge and awareness and in encouraging parents to request that schools continue some form of contact à la Portage if they so wish. There is a need therefore to provide facilities and attitudes to meet the increasing desire and expectations of parents which Portage fuels by the nature of its involvement.

Portage therefore should never be seen as a means to a cut in pre-five provision by it being looked upon as a substitute. Indeed the contrary is true. The seminar group generally felt that in order for nurseries to respond to parents and become more closely involved in liaison and partnership, there was a need for larger numbers of mainstream nurseries, and for a teaching profession therein that is not stretched, overworked, underpayed and undervalued but is supported, recognized and given higher pay and status in order that the necessary links with the local community can take place.

Acknowledgements

The authors wish to thank all people involved in the Bradford and Keighley Portage scheme; in particular Judith Barras, senior social worker, for her continuing involvement in all aspects of Portage, Terence Wakelin, educational psychologist, for his continued support and for his work in the initial pilot study, Barbara Hall for her clerical and administrative support and Dr Barnardo's, Keighley, for their continuing involvement.

Editors' note: Paul Wiehl and Patsy Barrow present a very full and comprehensive account of the Portage activities in Bradford and Keighley and their title for the chapter belies the amount of work that has gone on over an approximate three-year period from October 1982.

Many Portage services up and down the country have started with a pilot project and Portage in Bradford was no exception. Starting 'small' has many advantages and certainly places less strain on limited finances and human resources. As with previous chapters in this book Wiehl and Barrow have illustrated how enthusiasm and support for Portage can grow despite adversity. Having two pilot projects to compare and contrast the authors had a full source of data.

Having presented an historical account of Portage in Bradford the training of volunteers becomes the major theme of the chapter. The content of the training days reflects careful thought to meet the needs of a very mixed group of participants. In keeping with the fundamental Portage principles of partnership the work in Bradford reflects a dismissal of the professionals as experts and concentrates rather on support and collective involvement.

Ironically, though, the authors in this chapter present an account of their work and the work of others which shows a high level of professional expertise and commitment.

An Evaluation of the Leicestershire Portage Training Scheme

Angela Holland and Joyce Scaife

Early intervention schemes

A number of authorities, including the 1978 Warnock Report, stress the importance of early intervention for the handicapped child. Early intervent-ion schemes may take various forms and in the UK the model of service for many handicapped pre-school children tends to be home-based with the centre-based services running concurrently (e.g. assessment centres). The Portage model has become a popular home visiting service and the number of these schemes has increased during recent years. The need for the evaluation of such schemes is evident and Reader (1984) emphasizes the need for better documentation of pre-school programmes to overcome gaps in knowledge and to individualize services to parents and children.

Various authors have reported the outcome of Portage schemes. Overall, these studies suggest positive results. Outcome measures have differed considerably from scheme to scheme, but tend to focus on (i) the child's developmental progress as assessed by the Portage checklist, activities achieved, or by progress on a standardized assessment procedure, or (ii) parental satisfaction with the scheme, or (iii) skills gained and effected by staff trained in Portage methodology.

Revill and Blunden (1978) assessed the impact of a Portage service in South Glamorgan by means of the Portage checklist, Griffiths Mental Development Scale and by questionnaires issued to parents. A service was delivered to 19 children aged from 18 months to 4 years whose initial scores on the Griffiths Scale ranged from 8 to 89 (mean 100). Group A consisted of nine clients and group B of ten clients; evaluation measures were taken for a two-month baseline period for group A and a four-month baseline period for group B. Assessment was made at two-monthly intervals throughout the baseline and evaluation period. The questionnaire was issued to 16 mothers eight months after the first baseline measures were taken. Results showed an increase in mean Portage checklist skills gained per month from 4.2 and 3.7 in the baseline period to 11.1 and 9.4 in the evaluation period for group A and B respectively. The mean number of points on the Griffiths Mental Development Scale increased from 1.0 and 0.4 to 4.1 and 2.7 per two months for group A and B respectively, although the authors point out that individual children showed much variation on this measure and not all children showed consistent gains. Results of the parental questionnaire showed very favourable attitudes towards the scheme.

Smith *et al.* (1977) describe the Wessex Portage project in which 13 children took part in the first six months. 82 per cent of the activities set were successful and all children, regardless of skill level, attained success on a high proportion of activity charts set for them. The parents (particularly mothers) were generally enthusiastic about the home teaching project and this may have reflected in the finding that families were almost invariably home for arranged home visits. Similar results were found by Blunden (1982), i.e. 88 per cent of activities set were achieved and the service was well received by parents. Holland and Noaks (1982) used the Malaise Inventory (Rutter, 1970) with 14 families involved in the Portage scheme in mid-Glamorgan. The results showed a reduction in depression from 29 per cent to 21 per cent following the Portage intervention for six months.

Few studies have investigated the long-term effects of a Portage service. Clements *et al.* (1981) reported that out of 30 children receiving the service, four were placed in ordinary schools and 23 attended an assessment centre for special education. However, the evaluation of the long-term outcome presents methodological and ethical problems, e.g. the use of a control group design would not be acceptable over a long period. In addition, children enter schemes at different ages, and the criteria for acceptance varies.

Various factors may account for the success of reported Portage projects. The Portage approach involves parents in the teaching process and in deciding what to teach their child and this can be valuable for both parent and child. Many authors report the importance of parental involvement, e.g. Holland and Noaks (1982). Other factors in the Portage approach may also contribute towards its success, e.g. the structure offered within the goal-planning approach, monitoring within the system, the multi-disciplinary approach. In addition, the service is home based which has many advantages, e.g. reduction of anxiety for both parent and child. However, other studies (Clements *et al.*, 1982) report the successful use of Portage in other settings such as day nurseries, although some modification of the approach has been considered necessary.

Although many of the findings concerning Portage are positive, some notes of caution have been sounded. Wishart, Bidder and Gray (1980) found that families with Down's syndrome children and those with less severe delays prefer their children to receive day care. Families with a more severely handicapped child may require more material help. In addition, it may be questioned whether it is wise to turn parents into teachers and so perhaps transform the uniqueness of parents' natural interactions with their child. Sloper *et al.* (1983) interviewed parents of Down's syndrome infants who were receiving different 'intensities' of intervention (not Portage), and found that many parents of children aged 18 months or more preferred a less intensive approach and began to show resistance to a direct teaching approach. In addition, the need for flexibility within the programme was emphasized.

It is suggested that further research is required in the area of early intervention schemes, particularly in relation to mentally handicapped children and their families. The current study offers additional data in support of enhanced development for children receiving a Portage service.

Portage in Leicestershire

The Portage scheme as it is implemented in Leicestershire follows much the same model as reported in other schemes throughout the country (e.g. Smith *et al.*, 1977, Revill and Blunden, 1978).

Home visiting is provided by professional staff primarily from health education and the voluntary sector from within existing resources; each home visitor taking one or two families in addition to their existing case-load. Weekly visits are made to families and there is weekly attendance at a support/supervision meeting with the clinical psychologist supervisors. Referral to the scheme is made through the community health system. Children are required to meet the criteria of being Down's syndrome; attending less than 2½ days away-from-home placement and living within a designated catchment area.

Method

The scheme was implemented in January 1982 with the progress of the first 12 cases being closely monitored as a pilot study with a view to amassing further evidence as to the effectiveness of Portage in general and its effects locally in particular. The first six cases (group A) were assessed on referral and again six months later. The second six children referred (group B) were placed with parental agreement, on a waiting list. They were assessed on referral, after six months on the waiting list, and after six months receiving the scheme. The assessments made were criterion-referenced through Portage materials, norm referenced by the Bayley Scale of Mental Development, and by analysis of video-tapes of parents in a free-play situation with their child. This chapter reports the results achieved from assessment by Portage materials and Bayley Scale scores over the first two years of the scheme.

The children

By December 1984, 29 children had been referred to the scheme of whom 25 met the criteria for inclusion. Table 1 summarizes what happened to these 25 children.

Table 1: Details of children referred in the first two years of Portage

Number of children	Position at December 1984
14	currently on scheme
2	newly allocated; visits about to commence
3	visited until attended nursery/nursery school
1	allocated nursery place prior to visits commencing
3	moved out of catchment area
2	died.

Home visitors

During the time in which the scheme had been in operation, home visitors have left and been replaced by staff from either the same or different disciplines. In December 1984 there were ten active home visitors, comprising three peripatetic teachers for pre-school children with special needs, two community nurses for the mentally handicapped, two Church of England children's home staff, one specialist health visitor and one member of staff from Mencap. There have been recurrent difficulties in maintaining staffing of the scheme at the required level as the scheme has been run by the goodwill of the professions and agencies involved. Attempts are being made to gain funding for the scheme and involve a wider range of disciplines.

Activities set at November 1984

During the first two years of operation of the scheme a total of 968 activities were set. 87 per cent of these were achieved within one week. A trend for the target to be achieved later in the week has continued over the duration of the scheme with 53 originally being achieved on day 1 and 26 per cent being achieved on the first day of November 1984.

Portage checklist skills gained

There are many difficulties inherent in the use of the Portage checklist to evaluate differential rates of progress for children prior to, and whilst receiving, Portage visits. Of primary importance is the fact that there is no uniformity between the number of items per age range or between different sections of the checklist. It may be that a child attains a greater number of checklist skills at any one time because there are more items available in that particular age range of the checklist. Nevertheless, data for the waiting list control group shows a tendency for an increased rate of checklist skills to be gained during the period of active visiting (Table 2).

Table 2: Checklist skills gained by waiting list control group

child	age at first assessment (months)	skills gained in 6 m waiting period	skills gained in 6 m active visiting
1	2.2	47 (largely motor and socialization)	52 (evenly spread)
2	1.8	29	44
3	3.1	30	68
4	admitted to day nursery		
5	1.7	55	87
6	1.4	n/a	82 (4 months)

NB This data is not comparable with that of Revill and Blunden (*op. cit.*) as it is based on the Leicestershire revised language checklist.

Psychometric testing

Initially, Bayley Scale data were examined by comparing the months of mental age gained during the period prior to the Portage service being delivered and mental age gained during active visiting. For practical reasons it proved impossible to test children exactly six months from the preceding date of testing thus making comparison difficult. Data have thus been translated into mean months of mental age gained per calender month and the results are summarized in tabular form below (Tables 3 and 4).

Table 3: Mean mental age gains per month (Bayley Scale) for group A

child	pre-Portage	after approx 6 m of home visiting
1	0.77	0.83
2	0.83	0.79
3	0.10	0.25
4	0.50	0.52
5	0.66	0.66
6	0.63	0.59

During the waiting period, it appears as if the children's rate of development as assessed by the Bayley Scale of Mental Development slowed down, subsequently being maintained or showing a reverse after the introduction of the Portage scheme. Carr (1975) suggests that the IQ of children with Down's syndrome decreases with age, and the current results may be viewed optimistically in this light.

Table 4: Mean mental age gains per month (Bayley Scale) for group B

child	initial assessment	end of waiting period	after approx 6 m of home visiting
1	0.80	0.60	0.53
2	0.58	0.54	0.53
3	0.56	0.53	0.54
4	0.62	0.50	admitted to day nursery
5	0.70	0.57	0.68
6	0.41	0.41	0.59

NB Mean score for the general population is 1.0.

Limitations

Whilst the above results are encouraging and add to the literature on the positive benefits of Portage home visiting, conclusions are nevertheless limited by almost unsurmountable methodological problems inherent in clinical studies. Data were collected and analysed by the psychologists supervising the scheme and only brief follow-up was possible. Nevertheless, comparisons are made across time periods during which other professional intervention was available to the families which suggests additional benefits conferred by home visiting schemes.

It is also clear that some families benefit more from this type of service than others. A choice of services is necessary, as is an investigation of factors influencing a child and family's likely benefit from each of the available service options.

Editors' note: Holland and Scaife have developed the theme of evaluation by presenting data generated from Portage work in the Leicestershire Portage scheme.

The authors' evaluation extends over the first two years of the scheme and is therefore longer term than some of the previous pilot studies.

In a clear presentation of data and subsequent analysis, the authors reflect on the difficulties of evaluating Portage service deliveries in general and their own in particular. They present us with further questions about where we go from here, but imply that greater flexibility and choice needs to be a feature of future service deliveries.

The Implications of Research for the Future Development of Portage

Peter Sturmey

The family

At the centre of Portage is the key notion that parents are able and willing to undertake regular teaching of their mentally handicapped child at home. This is enshrined in the phrase *partnership with parents*. However our ideas of what families are and how they relate to a handicapped member are often based more on ideals and shared stereotypes of what families *should* be like rather than on reality (Turnbull and Turnbull, 1982).

Parents' involvement with a mentally handicapped child may vary from rejection at birth, to desire to help their child to the best of their ability, through to becoming excessively involved with their child to the exclusion of many other activities. Given the range of desirability and time for involvement with their child parents would be best served with a variety of service options of which home-based teaching by parents would be one choice.

Parents often have many demands placed upon them other than their mentally handicapped child. The presence of other dependent family members such as elderly, physically handicapped, chronically sick or mentally ill persons may determine the amount of time and energy they are able to invest in their mentally handicapped child. The presence of other children may help or hinder the process of teaching. If there are several young children all close together in age this may place too great a burden on parents. However, a young brother or sister may provide a very effective model for many years to assist in teaching the mentally handicapped child. Similarly, teenage brothers and sisters may be valuable in actively assisting in home-based teaching.

Although partnership with parents is often talked of, the care of a dependent family member frequently falls on women and most home-based teaching is carried out by mothers. Although little studied within Portage, other home-based teaching services have found that some maternal characteristics predict the extent to which teaching is carried out. If the mother is poorly educated, not well trained in the methods of teaching, socially isolated, depressed, or poor, then she is less likely to carry out home-based teaching without extra help (Cullen *et al.*, 1981; Dumas and Wahler, 1983; Griest *et al.*, 1983). Thus understanding the skills and resources of the mother appears to be crucial in home-based teaching.

Possible solutions

If the range of resources and needs of the families are recognized then it follows that a wide range of provision should be made, tailored carefully to the needs and resources of families. Portage would be one of these options. Other options that exist include day nurseries which may include Portage-style teaching (Clements *et al.*, 1982) and may involve parent participation (Goodman *et al.*, 1984). Other forms of intervention such as respite care may help parents under a lot of stress. Parents who are socially isolated may benefit from help to find social support and advice on how to use available social support to the full (Barsh *et al.*, 1983). Other families may benefit more from help directed at tackling the problems of chronic poverty (Heber and Garber, 1975).

None of these solutions necessarily excludes Portage. However as early intervention services continue to expand they may form both useful supplements to Portage and viable options for those families who do not get the most out of Portage.

Choosing goals

Choosing goals for teaching is at the heart of all forms of goal planning and yet it is often given little careful consideration. The common method is to assess the child on a behavioural checklist and select one of the next items off the checklist. Choosing goals is rarely as simple as this. Several goals may be 'next' on separate scales of the checklist and it is not often clear which goal should be chosen. Although the Portage checklist (Bluma *et al.*, 1976) is a useful point of departure for selecting goals it does have a number of problems if it is to be used for this. Other factors need to be considered.

Goals are often not of equal significance for the child. For example learning to walk may have immediate advantages to a child whereas a goal such as 'Name five textures' may be of little day-to-day use. Parents often place different values on different goals. For example, the areas of self-help, language and problem behaviours are often more valued than areas such as leisure skills (Geiger *et al.*, 1978). A further factor to consider in selecting goals is in areas in which home visitors and parents have expertise in teaching. Teaching home visitors and parents a new teaching method may not be worthwhile for just one goal if they can already teach many other skills that are equally useful.

Consideration should also be given to the settings in which a child spends time. Certain settings are very tolerant of lack of skill whereas others may be intolerant. For example, incontinence may be easily tolerated at home; in public places this may not be so. Skills could be ordered in this way in order to help select goals for teaching. Some behaviours may be required in all settings – for example, not being aggressive to others. Other behaviours may be 'luxuries', i.e. desirable but not necessary and still other behaviours may be elastic, i.e. they may be required in some, but not other, settings.

When selecting a goal careful consideration should be given not only to the requirements of his or her present settings but also to settings which the child is likely to enter in the near future.

Finally, the notion of chronologically age-appropriate behaviour should also be considered. This is more usually discussed in relation to mentally handicapped adults where gross discrepancies between their actual age and the type of activities they sometimes participate in may be apparent. With under-fives this may be more difficult to establish, but it may be useful to consider at what age children typically participate in activities such as riding a bike, going swimming or playing with other children in order to avoid the problem of only selecting babyish goals.

Possible solutions

When selecting goals for home-based teaching careful consideration should be given to many factors – filling out the checklist is only one step in selecting a goal for teaching. Factors other than the developmental status of the child should be explicitly considered. They include the significance of goal for the child, the priorities of the parents, the areas of expertise in teaching of the home visitor and parent, the demands of the child's parent and future settings and the chronological age of the child. These different reasons for selecting a goal may conflict directly with one another and flexibility and compromise among them are often necessary.

Generalist training

Successful teaching by parents depends upon how well they are taught by home visitors during their weekly visits and the teaching methods suggested to parents by home visitors. Home visitors teach parents by a combination of modelling and verbal feedback on their performance as teachers; the activity acts as a prompt for parents' teaching behaviours in between visits.

There has only been one study which has investigated different methods of parent training specifically within the context of Portage. Bidder *et al.*, 1982 compared: (1) giving parents suggestions for teaching, (2) setting specific targets to be taught, and (3) a full activity chart. They found that although full activity charts made home visits longer than during the other two methods, children made greatest progress with this method.

Surprisingly little other research has been done on parent training within Portage although an enormous amount has been done in comparing different methods of parent training during other home-based services. One important issue has been the relative effectiveness of modelling compared to generalist training in behaviour modification. Training parents by modelling how to teach specific tasks can be highly successful; parents gain skills and the child may learn. However, generalization of parent teaching skills to teaching other tasks may be very poor and can lead to slower gains by the child. When parents are given training in the *general* principles of behaviour modification then parents may be able to tackle teaching a wide range of different tasks to their child successfully without the need for home visitors to model every task (Koegel *et al.*, 1978; McMahon *et al.*, 1981).

Possible solutions

It may be feasible to change the method of training parents from modelling to a more generalist training in behavioural methods of teaching. Thus, during home visits emphasis would be placed on the application of general teaching skills (reinforcement, prompting, fading, punishment) to a particular goal that had been selected. It would be important to evaluate such a change in the method of training parents experimentally before it was more generally implemented. As noted before, any one form of intervention is unlikely to suit all people equally. There may be some parents who acquire more teaching skills through modelling and/or who prefer modelling to a more generic approach.

If a more generic approach were taken to training of parents there would be important implications for home visitors. Learning behavioural teaching methods is a complex and demanding set of skills and the idea that home visitors can be taught all that is necessary in one week is a myth (Dessent, 1984). If home visitors are to assist parents in learning and applying generalist skills then they too must receive greater support from supervisors. One possibility would be more detailed training of home visitors in behaviour modification (e.g. Foxen and McBrien, 1981). At this point it is worth noting the home visitors often give families help in ways other than carrying out home-based teaching. Liaising with and providing information about other services and dealing with family problems are just two areas in which home visitors may require further training and support.

Further research

At this point I shall not go into great detail about studies which have attempted to evaluate Portage. Most of these studies are published and available (Revill and Blunden, 1979; Shearer and Shearer, 1972; Clements *et al.*, 1982; Sandow *et al.*, 1981). Instead I should like to delineate what I view as key areas of future research.

Almost all research to date has focused on the child, namely on the rate of goals set and achieved or changes in IQ. This has usually been done by traditional experiment and control group design or a time-series design. In effect such projects have posed the question 'Does Portage change IQ or rate of goal acquisition?' I should like to argue that this is an over-simplistic question. It is unlikely that *any* one form of early intervention will help all children and their families in the same way. Children and their families are very diverse. Gray and Wanderson (1980) rephrased the question as follows: 'What characteristics of home-based interventions are effective in facilitating which areas of competence for which members of the families in which social contexts?'

Possible solutions

Research on Portage should take a far broader view of the possible effects of Portage on the child and the family. The measures used to evaluate Portage focused on the child. Future efforts could widen this perspective to look at a broader range of outcome measurers both of the child (e.g. the child's performance at school, changes in problem behaviours) and the family (e.g. consumer satisfaction, compliance with the intervention, attitudes and expectations of the child, divorce-rate, effects on siblings). An important implication of Gray and Wanderson's view is that instead of looking for main effects of treatment we should look at the interactions between type of early intervention (eg home- versus centre-based) and other factors (e.g. amount of family distress, urban versus rural area).

A second area, badly in need of evaluation, is the set of materials developed for use during Portage. Very little is formally known about them but some dissatisfaction with them exists since other materials, both for assessment and staff training, have been developed. Materials vary in their ease of reading and the degree to which they promote compliance with home-based teaching. As yet neither the original nor new materials have been compared and evaluated.

A third important area for research is the long-term effects of early intervention. Several studies have shown that although considerable acceleration of intellectual gains is feasible for mildly handicapped individuals, these gains may not be maintained long into the school years. Other effects may be found during early adulthood, although this is controversial (Gray *et al.*, 1982). The transition from Portage into a day nursery or school requires careful planning and liaison if gains made during Portage are to be maintained and continued. Long-term follow-up on Portage is badly needed.

Portage Guide to Early Education: recommendations

Portage has come a long way from its first implementation in the late 1960s. Over that period of time it has developed in a number of ways. It is therefore apt to consider some important features of the original Portage before suggesting ways in which Portage might develop in the future.

The original scheme took place in a rural area of the United States where a centre-based project was impractical due to transport problems. A home-based project was therefore chosen. Families entered the project by volunteering following advertisements in the local media. The mean IQ of the children was 75. Most of them would not therefore be considered mentally handicapped and there would have been few severely or profoundly mentally handicapped children. Portage has not now only crossed the Atlantic but is also used with children with a wider range of handicapping conditions than it was originally designed for. It now caters for families who are usually referred to the service by outside agencies rather than request the service.

Recommendation 1

Portage is now widely used in the United Kingdom and must therefore be feasible and acceptable to many consumers. This fact cannot be readily dismissed. Portage is here to stay. However, no service remains static. If the diversity of children and their families is fully recognized then the present Portage model will be extended, modified, and supplemented with other early intervention services to meet this diverse need.

Recommendation 2

Portage uses a home-based model of service delivery. This may suit some, but not all families. In urban areas it is possible to implement both centre- and home-based services. Centre-based services such as day nurseries and respite might benefit highly stressed families more than home-based services by providing respite for the families and teaching carried out by relatively unstressed professionals.

Recommendation 3

Some consumer dissatisfaction with the Portage materials has arisen as evidenced by the development of new materials. These materials could be assessed in terms of their readability, consumer satisfaction and compliance, reliability across time, testers and informants, and the validity of the scales.

Recommendation 4

The training of both parents and home visitors has been comparatively limited. Training of parents has focused on modelling particular tasks rather than more general skills. Training of home visitors has focused principally on teaching behavioural skills to parents rather than the wider range of problems that they have to tackle. Training of parents could be focused on training them in general skills of behavioural training although this requires careful comparison with modelling. Training of home visitors could involve more thorough training of behavioural teaching methods than hitherto and be broadened to cover dealing with other frequently encountered problems.

Editors' note: Peter Sturmey's chapter presents a useful analysis of present day information with regard to the implications of a Portage service delivery upon the family, parental training, choice of teaching goals and evaluation techniques.

His chapter presents further areas for future research and possible solutions to problems in such a positive manner that the reader can feel inspired to go out and identify more effective ways of combating the problems that are highlighted. For the more committed researcher this author does in fact share a range of research topics which are awaiting investigation.

In the introduction to his chapter the author reports that 'one of the strengths of Portage is that it continually evaluates itself in order to make constructive changes.' Indeed this is the case and other chapters in the book provide details of such evaluation from a variety of projects. Nevertheless, as Peter Sturmey rightly describes, much of the evaluation has been confined to the progress of the child and a much wider view is required.

The editors' belief is that limited research up to press may be due in large part to lack of financial and human resources. Many of the authors in this book have identified problems in their projects relating to lack of, or, insecure funding.

Hopefully the extension of Portage projects around the country in response to the ESG money will generate both enthusiasm and finances to pursue a wider range of research topics that Peter Sturmey has so ably brought to our attention. He emphasizes throughout his chapter the need for flexibility in responding to the needs of parents and children with special needs and future researchers must take this important notion into consideration.

Pilot into Portage in Worcester Health District

Susan Richards and Sheila Hallows

Prior to Portage, Worcester, like most districts, had certain provisions for handicapped children. Basically this consisted of an assessment centre and further follow-up to this in a nursery unit to the age of five years if considered necessary. After that age there were three special schools for placement depending on the type and severity of the handicap. These were well supported by the paediatric service. The school health service provided further developmental assessment and follow-up.

The health visiting service has always placed great emphasis on the detection and follow-up of any deviation from the norm, both physical and mental. The health visitor is admirably placed for this task due to his or her close proximity to the family which commences in the ante-natal period and continues from the 11th day post-natally up to school age and beyond.

Following the detection of early handicap, the mode of referral could take the following forms:

1. Referral to general practitioner, who referred in turn to the paediatrician, who may involve other paramedical services, e.g. physiotherapy, speech therapy, psychological and others as necessity dictated.
2. Referral to clinical medical officer, who may involve the same professionals as listed above or may directly use the local services available, e.g. special playgroups to meet the individual needs of that child.

Worcester district did have some insight into the shortcomings with regard to providing help for mentally handicapped children and had gone some way towards bridging this gap, by setting up parent workshops to provide some practical help to parents. These support groups were not found to be entirely satisfactory because parents tended to compare their children and various professionals often gave conflicting advice through inadequate knowledge of behaviour patterns in handicapped children. As a result of the Warnock report, a type of Portage had been introduced in Worcester as far back as the 1970s. This had been set up by an educational psychologist and a teacher in one of the special assessment nurseries, but this seedling enterprise did not flourish for various reasons. The big drawback with all the existing schemes in the district seemed to be the lack of education given to the parents in handling their handicapped child in their own home and the parents therefore lacked awareness, understanding and knowledge of how to intervene on their child's behalf in order for the child to reach his or her full potential.

Discussions about Portage in Worcester district began as a result of a meeting held in November 1981 at Lea Hospital – a hospital specializing in the care of the mentally handicapped. Interested professionals in the immediate vicinity were invited to share ideas and schemes. It was appreciated that the Portage model cut across all professionals and there were representatives from:

Community nursing (mental handicap)
Health visiting
Psychology (educational and clinical)
Education
Social services

Following that meeting a smaller group of people in Worcester district began meeting on a regular basis to discuss in greater detail how a Portage scheme could be started in the district.

At that time, similar schemes had been set up and had been successfully running in Wessex, South Wales and Lancashire, to name a few and it was interesting to note that the demand for a Portage home advisory service had already been coming from parents moving into the district from such areas where the schemes were already in operation. As an outcome of discussion it was noted that there were many members of staff in the district, who were interested in being trained and using Portage, including community nurses (mental handicap), clinical psychologists and health visitors.

They fall into one of two groups. Those who knew already of Portage in other districts and had either read or come into contact with a scheme and had been impressed by its results and those who had little or no idea about Portage but who were desperately anxious to fill the growing gaps in their expertise with handling handicapped children.

As a result of meetings held over several months, it was proposed that a Portage scheme should be set up in Worcester health district. The general consensus was that it should start in a small way and gradually build up expertise. Shortly after this a Portage management team was set up in Worcester. This had a multi-disciplinary membership and its chief function was to coordinate the scheme across geographical areas and professions with specific tasks in organizing training, appointing staff, obtaining resources.

The management team consisted of clinical psychologists, speech therapists, senior medical officers, occupational therapists, paediatricians, physiotherapists, nurse representatives for health visiting and community nursing in mental handicap and representatives from education. These were all at senior management level in order to enable discussion of services in general.

The initial task of this management team was to compile a list of potential users of the service and draw up criteria which would be used to assess appropriateness for inclusion in the scheme; eventually they had further functions. In the early stage, it was suggested that three small groups of home advisory teams should be established, each one to cover a small geographical area – Worcester city, Wychavon and Malvern. Initially it was envisaged that each team would have one family which would be visited once a week for one hour during the pilot phase, in which staff could gradually build up their skills.

The proposed development of this model was that each home adviser team would gradually grow in size by taking on extra home advisers. It was envisaged that clinical psychologists would adopt the supervisor roles and coordinate the teams. The independent home advisers would gradually increase their case load and this would allow a controlled build up of the scheme and would enable new recruits to spend some time in an in-service training position attached to one member of the team. There were obviously many general issues to be resolved. In the first instance:

1 *Referrals* It was felt essential that eventually self-referrals from families would be accepted, but initially pilot families were likely to be chosen on an individual basis and that later it would be the task of the management team to develop a set of criteria for inclusion in the Portage scheme and then draw up a list of all clients eligible for the service. In considering the criteria, there were certain essential ingredients, e.g. age (0 – 5), geographical area, current use of other services, level of ability and type of handicap.

Table 1: The Portage materials

Description	Quantity	Cost (1983)
Portage Guide to Early Education	11	10 at £56.95 1 at £59.95
Portage Parent Programme	10	9 at £11.95 1 at £14.95
British Manual for Implementing Portage Home Training Service	1	1 at £4.45
Working Together – Portage Conference Proceedings Book	4	4 at £5.95
Wessex Revised Portage Language Checklist	9	9 at £7.65
Activity Cards	9	9 at £5.95
Portage Guide to Home Teaching Book	10	9 at £6.95 1 at £8.95
	TOTAL	£974.10

2 *Clerical back up and physical space* This was a local issue, which was resolved by not necessarily having the same place for meetings on each occasion.
3 *Equipment* It was envisaged that each home advisory team should have one complete set of all Portage materials and books (see Table 1).
4 *Training* Before embarking on any home visiting, it was important that all those involved were adequately trained in the Portage method. This could be implemented in one of two ways: (a) everyone should attend a workshop outside the area, or (b) a Portage workshop should be set up in the locality for three days. In the end it was the latter method which was adopted.
5 *Evaluation* All the Portage home advisory schemes had been well evaluated in the USA and parts of this country and had been found to be an effective form of intervention. It was wisely considered that the Worcester Portage scheme should have an in-built means of evaluation both in terms of checklist recording progress and in monitoring the effectiveness of the scheme.

From then on Worcester was on its way to establishing a Portage home advisory service in the district and indeed theory was turned into realization when a total of £1,400 was allocated to the scheme.

Function of the management group

The function of the group was outlined as follows:

(a) Organization of a Portage service/administrative issues } in conjunction with appropriate unit managers.
(b) To ensure adequate financial resources.
(c) To decide on methods of referral and to receive the same.
(d) To establish criteria of eligibility of children for acceptance on the scheme.
(e) To set a procedure for selection.
(f) To receive reports from supervisors and monitor the provision of service.
(g) To monitor, with sector managers, staff performance and to provide staff with feedback on how well they are fulfilling the specific duties allocated.
(h) To organize basic training courses, as required, and to ensure a sound programme of on-going in-service training and availability of required teaching material.
(i) To review the need for equipment.

The new management team then undertook to set up (i) a workshop for the training of Portage advisers, and (ii) criteria for selection of families.

Selection criteria

As far as possible the following criteria were used in selecting children to take part in the scheme:

(a) Age $4\frac{1}{2}$ years or less but preferably young children of up to 18 months.
(b) *Not* attending nursery school or playgroup more than five half-days per week.
(c) A score of 78 or below on two sub-scales of the Griffiths scale.
(d) Living in the local community.
(e) No complicating features which are likely to impede progress.
(f) Parent(s) who are keen and interested to take on the commitment,

and the distribution of information to various heads of services who might be called upon for advice by the home advisory teams.

Evaluation of PPS

The evaluation measures were decided upon before the commencement of the service in accordance with agreed principles. These were as follows:

(i) Independant measure of function using the Griffiths scale
(ii) Portage checklist – a built-in evaluation
(iii) Consumer questionnaire
(iv) Details of diary

Training course

At the start of this project, health visitors and community nurses were asked to volunteer first to take a three-day in-service training course and following this, to agree to become home advisers for the pilot scheme.

In November 1983 a three-day basic training course was attended by community nurses, health visitors and representation from the teaching profession, clinical medical officers and nursery nurses.

The course tutor was Ms Sue Gardener, district clinical psychologist, East Berkshire Health Authority, an experienced Portage home adviser. Ms Gardener was supported by three clinical psychologists from Worcester health district to lead discussion group sessions.

The programme was as follows:

Day I

Introduction to Portage, its origin and development in the USA and now in Great Britain.

Portage materials – checklist and index card system
Parent/Instructor Manuals

Questioning parents – Interviewing technique

Choosing tasks

Day II

Behavioural objectives

Charts

Task analysis

Use of and recording on activity charts

Specimen charts written out and handed in for assessment and comment

Day III

Feedback to groups on recording activity charts

Counselling aspects in the home

Setting up the service – i.e. roles of management group
roles of supervision and supervisor
roles of home advisers
Role of the family health visitor in relation to the role of the home adviser.

Pilot scheme

Six health visitors, one community nurse (mental handicap) and three clinical psychologists were selected to take part in Worcester health district's pilot scheme. The clinical psychologists agreed to supervise the other members of the team at the same time as working with a child/parent themselves.

Role of the supervisor

(a) To act as a coordinator to the home advisory group
(b) To allocate children selected to a home adviser
(c) To act as liaison with the management group

(d) To have an assessment role as required
(e) To act as an adviser to the home adviser, discussing activity charts, etc.
(f) To assist with in-service training
(g) To undertake joint visits to families as required
(h) To provide and collate written reports to the management group or other professionals.

It was decided that each team would meet weekly for supervision to discuss each visit made by the home adviser. These would commence in January 1984 and would have the following objectives:

To learn about and understand Portage method
To review problems with setting new goals
To review any current problems with setting new tasks
To discuss referral to other agencies
To invite other involved professionals to come to meetings and offer input.

For the pilot study a number of children with a handicap were identified and forwarded by the family health visitor to the management group for selection. In each case the family health visitor had carried out a home visit to introduce the idea of Portage early teaching, and to discuss the family participation in the pilot scheme proposed.

The management group used the Glamorgan scheme criteria for eligibility:

1 Not more than 4½ years.
2 Not attending playschool or nursery.
3 Should score 78 or below, two standard deviations or less on more than one subtest of the Griffiths Mental Development Scale.
4 Should be living in a geographical catchment area.

The first meeting of all the home advisory teams was convened in January 1984 to discuss the venue for weekly meetings and staff availability.

An information leaflet describing Portage early teaching was sent to all the families selected.

Appointments for a head teacher of a special school were made (independent of home advisory staff) to visit the families in their homes. A structured interview then took place and a questionnaire was completed with the cooperation of the parents. This was designed to give some measure of parental attitudes towards their handicapped child and their expectations of the Portage service prior to its commencement. A repeat parallel questionnaire was completed under similar circumstances after the home visiting phase.

The home advisers also completed a questionnaire before the home visiting phase commenced, sampling experience and attitudes towards developmental delay and the Portage system and similarly after the home visiting phase.

Attitudes were assessed on a four-point scale labelled for example:

Confident
Fairly confident
Doubtful
Very doubtful

Each category could be clearly related to other categories on a 'greater than', 'less than', 'equals' basis even though the distance between the categories could not be defined. Data were thus on an ordinal scale of measurement.

Assessment of the children was undertaken by the clinical medical officer in a clinic base.

An assessment was also carried out with the Griffiths test. This has a standard deviation of 11 about a mean score of 100. Therefore a score of 78 represented two standard deviations below the mean. Children taken into Portage had to underscore on more than one section. If the underscore was in one area only the child would be referred for more specific help to the appropriate therapist (e.g. a delay in motor skills would be referred to the physiotherapist).

A medical check, including examination of growth, chest, hearing and vision, was also made.

The early weeks involved no home visiting until the clinical medical officers' assessments were completed. Reports went to all professionals involved and to the parents. Secretarial support and clerical work was discussed, and the home visiting diary and log sheet commenced. The importance of the accuracy of these records for evaluation purposes was stressed.

Clerical work for home advisers involved:

(a) Recording activity charts which were filled in in the home at each visit and collected the following week.
(b) Time sheets to be filled in weekly.
(c) Visiting diary to be filled in weekly.

Portage materials were supplied to the centres. Other equipment supplied were developmental assessment toys, e.g. bricks, crayons, puzzles and books. Contact with the local toy library was also made.

The home visiting phase was scheduled to start in February 1983 and to continue until December 1983 when the pilot scheme would be concluded for evaluation.

The family health visitor introduced the home adviser to the child and parent. In the early weeks the home adviser had the responsibility of setting up a positive learning environment in the home, keeping the visit business-like and strictly to Portage method, excluding the possibility of health visiting advice being sought by the family. If this did occur the family health visitor was asked to visit.

The Portage checklist was completed and task setting commenced.

The Portage checklist was reviewed in June and September and a progress report was written by the home adviser and copies were sent to the parent's general practitioner, family health visitor, management group and any other professional involved.

In July 1984 a senior nurse and the family health visitor visited all the families for an informal discussion to assess the acceptability of Portage service to the parents and children. Many parents felt they had benefited from the service. They valued the structured help and weekly visits from the home adviser and their supervision of their children's progress. Parents felt that having set goals helped them to teach their children in a positive way.

The Supervisors submitted an interim report to the management group.

The home visiting phase concluded in December 1984 and the second questionnaire was completed by the parents and home advisers.

A Griffiths assessment was carried out by clinical medical officers. The findings are reported below (Table 2).

Table 2: General Quotient Scores before and after the Portage year

Child	Before	After
1	27	15
2	84	81
3	68	62
4	76	74
5	52	43
6	78.5	66
7	30	37
8	53.4	55.6
9	76	69.6
10	22	16.6
MEAN	56.6	51.9

Answers to questionnaire I (parents) indicated that parents welcomed the Portage scheme, were confident in their abilities to teach their children at home and had high expectations of the scheme. Changes in parental attitude by the end of the scheme suggested an increase in confidence and more realistic expectations of their child's ability.

Questionnaire II (home advisers) suggested an increase in confidence in their abilities to achieve rapport with the child and to deliver an efficient service.

Advantages of Portage home advisery service to the child identified:
(a) Uses child's natural environment
(b) Individual approach
(c) Parents more focused on individual aims rather than getting bogged down by their child's whole handicap.

Advantages to the parent:
(a) Increases efficiency
(b) Increases parental confidence
(c) Strengthens emotional bond with child
(d) Convenience particularly if the parents have other children
(e) Benefits of feedback and objectivity.

Advantages to the services:
(a) Cost-effective – home base, parents become the teacher
(b) Removes the problem of failed clinic appointments
(c) Ensures utilization of professional advice
(d) Reduces instances of conflicting advice
(e) Monitors' need for other agencies.

On reflection of the project it is recommended that the training should include pre-training reading list and video samples of Portage in progress.

It was also felt that the newly trained home adviser should commence Portage home visiting with the supervisor. It is generally felt that fewer difficulties, e.g. writing the chart, identifying the goal, etc., would occur, and that this would help the newly trained home adviser to gain confidence in their newly acquired skills sooner. Joint visits between the home adviser and the supervisor should be repeated routinely at an agreed interval.

In an future training scheme all home advisers in training should have at least two joint visits in the first year.

Ideally a comprehensive toy library should be available at each base before the Portage service commences.

Portage continues to operate in Worcester health district and future training of staff is planned.

Conclusion

An attempt has been made to consider the setting up of a Portage scheme in Worcester health district and an evaluation of its working and effectiveness following a trial period of one year. Those of us who have persevered with the scheme have no doubt whatsoever of its effectiveness both for the child and parent.

Portage is a team approach towards a specific problem and in order to be effective each member of that team must be totally committed and enthusiastic.

Acknowledgements

Thanks to:
Portage management team, Worcester health district, for providing background information to the setting up of Portage in this district. Mrs A. Havas, sector nursing officer, for her help and support. The typist for all her hard work.

Editors' note: This chapter reports the setting up of a pilot Portage scheme.

Multi-disciplinary involvement at all levels is a key feature of the project and the roles of the Portage team and the criteria for acceptance of children on to the scheme are clearly identified.

Again in this chapter, as with others, the importance of training is emphasized and the contents of the three-day training course are described.

Evaluation appears to have been carefully thought out before the pilot was started and a variety of data were collected.

Ubiquitous optimism and commitment of these Portage workers comes over strongly as it does with the other schemes described in this book.

Evaluation – The Parental Perspective

Ewen Rennie

In a paper to the 1983 British Psychological Society Conference on 'Evaluating Portage' I concluded that:

> a combination of approaches will be necessary to give a full picture of the effectiveness of Portage. The two principal elements must be parental satisfaction and the success rate for activity charts but in the future measures of parental competence, locus of control and marital stability should help complete the picture. (Rennie, 1983)

In this chapter I consider the parental perspective as experienced by those parents of children in Kirklees who have had (or are having) Portage. Two separate 'measures' are reported. Firstly a postal questionnaire to all parents of children who had 'graduated' from the Kirklees Portage projects between July 1980 and June 1985 – 29 children in total. (The Postal Group.) (For responses see Appendix.) Secondly the results from a semi-structured interview of individual parents (whose children were currently receiving Portage) conducted by Sheila Arney and Janet Connolly during June 1984 when they were postgraduate students of educational psychology on placement in Kirklees. (I gratefully acknowledge permission to quote their results.) (The Present Group.)

Consumer satisfaction

In my original paper I suggested that one should occasionally ask parents whether they wished to continue with Portage and whether they would recommend Portage to other parents of children with special needs. Arney and Connolly did this for the then current Portage families and received approval for Portage on both counts from 13 of the 14 families.

Two items on the postal questionnaire also addressed themselves to the subject of consumer satisfaction. Question 3 asked parents to rate 'the most useful people to me in meeting my child's needs before school' and the answers show an overwhelming vote for Portage as against any other agency. The dubious statistic of a 'summed total of preference votes' gave Portage 48 points, 'parental support groups' and 'paediatrician' 20 points each, 'own family' 18 points, 'physiotherapist' 15 points and 'educational psychologist' 13 points. No other group attracted a minimum of five votes. It must be remembered, of course, that Portage is the common denominator of the group but even so it is clear that the Portage home visitor was, on reflection, a very important factor for these parents. Also significant is the fact that more parents rated a parent support group (ten votes) than any single professional. The two agencies also involved with every child (the family doctor and the health visitor) hardly attracted any votes. Only one parent mentioned a child assessment unit as an entity.

Another aspect of consumer satisfaction must be whether or not the model continues to be used after the home visitor has withdrawn. Question 4 on the postal questionnaire shows that 18 out of the 23 respondants continue to use the model at least occasionally. Over 75 per cent usage without the weekly stimulus shows the strength of the model. Five of the 14 present Portage group felt that Portage had helped them deal with/teach their other children. This of course raises the question of what do the consumers actually think Portage is all about.

The parental view of Portage

The postal group's responses to Question 1 shows a preponderance of parents believe Portage to be: 'A home teaching service aimed at increasing the skills of handicapped children' (14 'first' votes and 'summed total' of 47), with the favoured alternative being: 'Instructions to parents in teaching skills suitable for handicapped children' (seven 'first' votes and 'summed total' of 47). The role of the 'informed friend' is also valued by parents. This of course raises the question of 'has the child progressed?'

The parents' view of their child's progress

Certainly in the parents' eyes the majority of both the present and postal groups believe their child's progress has improved since being on Portage. In the Arney and Connolly group the results were:

The same – 2   Better – 8   Difficult to tell – 4

Amongst the postal group the results were even more strongly in favour of the developmental function of Portage with 17 claiming an improvement with Portage. Six of these felt that without Portage their child's progress would have been as good as it is now but would have taken longer in the initial stages, but the other 11 believed that without Portage their child's progress would have been poorer than it is now. (Only two parents believed that without Portage their child's progress would have been as good as it is now and no parents felt that Portage had hindered their child's development.)

Some of their comments express their feelings more eloquently:

> S went to a normal nursery and then to a normal school ... I sincerely believe that having Portage has helped her get there.
>
> We were both encouraged by the progress we were making with W and in our particular case the help received from Portage was invaluable.
>
> We feel it helped her on entering school and to carry on learning. (G is in a normal school.)
>
> Portage helped to prove H was capable of completing some tasks which we initially thought would be too difficult for him.
>
> Portage was the first 'positive' programme we received, positive in that our child began to 'achieve' instead of always being 'unable'.

Certainly these parents believe in Portage. So what do they think the long-term effect of Portage has been?

The effects of Portage

Two clear effects are seen by the parents: 'Improving his/her attention span, attitude to learning' (11 'first' choices, weighted vote '47') and 'Teaching me how to break things down into small steps to teach him/her' (nine 'first' choices, weighted total '43').

A third effect is preparation for school, whilst a significant minority of parents declared themselves as having gained in confidence in meeting with the professionals. It seems that Portage is definitely seen as educational (to both parents and child).

Conclusions

It can be argued that questionnaires are unreliable, subject to bias and influenced by temporal distortions in recall of previous development. Nevertheless the results reported here clearly show a high degree of consumer satisfaction. Parents like Portage!

As one parent put it:

> it gives you a lot of satisfaction knowing that you have achieved that yourself and that school is not the most important teaching aid around and that you can teach your children.

Would any school have achieved such positive results if it had posted out an evaluation questionnaire on itself? Would any psychological service be so praised by schools? I think not.

Portage works!

Acknowledgements

Thanks to:
Sheila Arney and Janet Connolly for permission to quote from their report.
Kath Jennings for assistance in the data collection.
The parents for their tolerance.

Editors' note: Ewen Rennie's chapter looks at the parental perspective in evaluating the effectiveness of a Portage service delivery. Data were collected from past and present Portage consumers.

Satisfaction is high amongst these parents but the author emphasized that this measure of evaluation is only one of a possible and necessary avenue of evaluative approaches to be made. This point has also been made by Peter Sturmey in his chapter. Ewen Rennie strongly indicates that psychological services in general could well consider extending and developing all aspects of their service delivery in order to please and satisfy clients at any level. This is an aspect which the editors would wish to encourage. Indeed there may be a strong case for extending all caring services so that they employ the model of regular visiting, with a clear idea of tasks required and goals set and of how the service is to be evaluated. If workers in all the caring agencies had such clarification of their role and function as in the Portage approach, how much easier it would be to evaluate and promote their usefulness to society.

Appendix: Responses to Parental Questionnaire

1 THE AIM OF PORTAGE IS TO PROVIDE

	Rating	*First*	*Second*	*Third*	*Summed Total*
a)	A home teaching service aimed at increasing the skills of handicapped children	14	6	3	57
b)	Regular visits from an 'informed' friend as a counselling service for parents	2	4	12	26
c)	Instructions to parents in teaching skills suitable for handicapped children	7	12	2	47
d)	An intermediary between parents and professionals	2	–	3	9
e)	Other	–	–	–	–

2 THE LONGEST LASTING EFFECT OF PORTAGE FOR MY CHILD HAS BEEN

	First	*Second*	*Third*	*Summed Total*
a) Improving the parent-child bond	–	3	2	8
b) Teaching me how to break things down into small steps to teach him/her	9	7	2	43
c) Giving me the confidence to meet with (and question) the professionals	–	2	9	13
d) Giving him/her the best possible start in school	3	4	4	21
e) Improving his/her attention span, attitude to learning	11	6	2	47
f) Other, please specify	–	–	–	–

3 ON REFLECTION THE MOST USEFUL PEOPLE TO ME IN MEETING MY CHILD'S NEEDS BEFORE SCHOOL WERE

	First	*Second*	*Third*	*Summed Total*
a) Paediatrician	5	1	3	20
b) Educational psychologist	2	2	3	13
c) Physiotherapist	4	1	1	15
d) Parent support group	3	4	3	20
e) Portage home visitor	9	8	5	48
f) My own family	3	3	3	18
g) Speech therapist	2	1	1	9
h) Family doctor	–	–	1	1
i) Occupational therapist	1	–	–	3
j) Ordinary playgroup	1	–	–	3
k) Health visitor	–	1	–	2

4 NOW THAT YOUR CHILD IS AT SCHOOL DO YOU STILL SET WEEKLY STEP-BY-STEP TEACHING GOALS

		Number
a)	Never	5
b)	Occasionally for tasks which he/she finds difficult	13
c)	At least one 'chart' per month	–
d)	Regular 'charts/goals'	5

5 IF YOU HAD NEVER RECEIVED PORTAGE WHAT DO YOU THINK YOUR CHILD'S PROGRESS WOULD HAVE BEEN

		Number
a)	Better than it is now	–
b)	As good as it is now	2
c)	As good as it is now but having taken longer in the initial stages	6
d)	Poorer than it is now	8
e)	Significantly poorer than it is now	3
f)	Don't know	4

Note: Above results based on responses of 23 parents. On Questions 1 and 3 one parent allocated three 'first' choices. Another allocated five first choices on question 3. Some third choices were not allocated.

The Rt. Hon. Sir Keith Joseph's Speech to the National Portage Association

Sir Keith Joseph's speech is recorded in this chapter as it was presented to the Conference of the National Portage Association in September 1985. The National Portage Association members were delighted that Sir Keith Joseph chose to attend and address the National Portage Conference. Many in the audience were employed as teachers and were therefore well aware of the pressure that the then Secretary of State was under at the time in view of the difficult situation with regard to the teachers' salary negotiations. Sir Keith Joseph faced an audience in Huddersfield of over 200. The audience consisted of parents with handicapped children, professionals from all parts of the education service and professionals who represented many other disciplines. Sir Keith Joseph grasped the cooperative and highly motivated atmosphere of the Conference immediately and before he delivered his speech he used audience participation to involve his audience fully in an appropriate dialogue. In this way he absolutely captured the spirit of cooperation and communication that is embodied in Portage. He addressed his audience and asked if there were parents present, if there were speech therapists present, if there were clinical medical officers present and encouraged various professionals in the audience to identify themselves. Using light humour and encouraging words he raised the whole atmosphere in the audience and contributed to making his speech one of the many highlights of the National Conference which cannot wholly be captured in a book such as this. Of course there was one other major highlight in that he announced the award of 1.2 million pounds to local authorities in England for the provision of multi-professional Portage-type teams to support parents in the education of children under five with special educational needs. The National Portage Association was also extremely flattered to be well praised by Sir Keith Joseph for its role in the development of Portage services throughout the country. As the National Portage Association had been fully constituted for just one year this praise was extremely well received by both the committee and all the members of the National Portage Association. Sir Keith Joseph's comments also provided further indication of the government's feeling about parental involvement in the educational development of their own children. Such involvement is seen as desirable as a positive contribution. After all, parents are the ones who know their own children best. Sir Keith Joseph sees Portage as a useful means of assessing and providing for a wider range of children's needs and he links the Portage service delivery with the obligations the local education authorities have in respect of young children under the 1981 Education Act. Sir Keith Joseph like Peter Sturmey and other authors in this book see Portage as an exciting and important aspect both of, and for the progressive change in education and development of young children.

It seems appropriate as an introduction to this chapter to include a little more about the education support grants. As Sir Keith Joseph points out, the grants will be available for three years up to 1991. In essence, up to £28,000 a year on 1985 figures is available to each local authority in England for setting up or extending and developing an existing Portage service. This chapter is thus in line with the theme of the book – 'extending and developing Portage'. The money will be available for a three-year period at the end of which the expectation is that the local authority will continue financing the newly set up service. The National Portage Association is recommending that the money should be used to appoint a senior Portage worker and at least one home visitor. The home visitor could be from a number of disciplines such as an NNEB nursery nurse or another related profession. It might interest readers to know that the Kirklees Portage service employs one part-time educational psychologist (Kath Jennings) and three part-time home visitors, and one part-time clerical assistant. The educational psychologist allocates 15 hours of the week to the Portage scheme and the other members of staff are employed for exactly half-time which in 1985 was 18½ hours per week. The cost of salaries, travelling expenses to the parents' homes and incidental office equipment, materials and other costs is approximately £28,000 and the Kirklees Portage project is able to service 23 families. The home visitors have a variety of backgrounds. One was an infant teacher, another was a nurse, and yet another had a background in nursery nursing.

The Department of Education and Science assumed that approximately 35 new projects would be set up each year and therefore hoped that over the initial three-year period most local education authorities in England would have a Portage service which would be able to help the local authority meet the obligations that the authority has under the 1981 Education Act. The allocation of the £28,000, which was the maximum allocation in 1986, was also intended to cover initial training and administration costs. Initially only one application per local education authority would be considered. The other important point to note is that the local education authorities when submitting an application were expected to demonstrate that multi-disciplinary cooperation was a feature of the proposal. The National Portage Association strongly recommends that the management level with representatives from health, social services and education should be an important component of any new service. It is envisaged that as the managers are employed anyway this would not particularly increase the costs for the service. Another important criterion was that the proposers must demonstrate the project will fulfil most of the components of the Portage model as described in the documents produced by the National Portage Association. The Department of Education and Science circular relating to the education support grant was sent to local education authorities in July 1985. Many local authorities received confirmation in January 1986 that their submission for a grant had been approved. There still will be an opportunity for other local authorities who have not yet submitted an application for an eduction support grant to do so in 1987 or 1988. The appropriate part of the circular which was received by local education authorities in July 1985 is reproduced here for information (see Appendix). It is an important milestone in the extension and development of Portage and therefore it is appropriate that it is included in this book. The editors are extremely grateful to Sir Keith Joseph for allowing us to record such a significant development in the extension and development of the services and we too look forward very much to the model extending into schools and indeed into other social services.

SIR KEITH JOSEPH'S SPEECH TO THE NATIONAL PORTAGE ASSOCIATION ON 7TH SEPTEMBER 1985

General opening remarks

I would like to thank you very much for the invitation to attend the National Portage Association. I am particularly glad to have the opportunity to address the association this year in view of the recent decisions to include Portage-type projects among the priorities for support under the Education Support Grant Act. When discussing ways of improving special education I frequently ask officials at the department what we can learn from other countries. I am delighted that on this occasion we can make use of and help to develop one of the systems that has its origins in the United States of America. Portage originated from the town of that name in Wisconsin. Portage programmes have an important contribution to make to the pattern of provision for children under five with special educational needs. The 1981 Education Act sets great store by cooperation between providing authorities and between professionals. There is a long history of separate responsibilities and against this background developing such cooperation is hard, especially at a time when resources are tight. It is difficult to allay the suspicion that one service is trying to get another to meet part of its expenditure. But the 1981 Act is about cooperation and communication: between schools and local education authorities, between parents and teachers, between parents and other professionals, and between professionals and local authority officials. Portage, like other developments in early education including nursery education, special education and playgroup provision, fosters all these. Portage is also designed to meet the needs of children below compulsory school age. This is an age range for which local education authorities have had statutory responsibilities since 1944, but the 1981 Act makes these duties more specific. Not only must authorities assess children over two where these children have been brought to their attention as having, or possibly having, special educational needs, they may also do so for children under two with the parents' consent. Early identification is very important but its justification lies in making suitable provision. This has been recognized for years in the case of the hearing impaired. The potential, however, is much wider if we carry the parents with us.

The government believes the Portage approach has a contribution to make to the range of provision offered to parents of young children with special needs and the children themselves. The growth in the numbers of schemes in the past few years underlines the positive response of parents to this method of meeting the needs of a wide variety of such children. It is perhaps worth pausing a while to reflect on the reasons for this success.

First, the scheme is flexible. The approach can be adapted to help children with many kinds of disability, including those with emotional and behavioural disturbances. It can be introduced when they are still very young. Even the most severely multiply handicapped children can benefit.

Secondly, and perhaps crucially, it provides a vital role for parents. Usually no one knows a child as well as his or her parents. The teaching role the scheme offers enables parents to make a positive contribution to monitoring and helping their child's development. So often parents are left looking on and feeling helpless, or even guilty, while professionals work with their child. By enabling them to work with the professionals as partners, parents not only help their child to make real progress, they also acquire confidence in their own abilities to work with their child. Some parents even develop skills to work with other children by becoming home visitors. This too is of great value to new parents.

Thirdly, the strength of the teams lies in the multi-professional composition. Mutual support and advice for home visitors contributes greatly to the method's success.

Fourthly, the scheme provides for proper management and supervision and for adequate administrative support. These, too, are vital to the successful introduction and running of the teams. The resulting records of progress for each child can make an invaluable contribution both to assessment procedures under the 1981 Act where these are necessary, and for teachers when the child transfers to school.

The government would like to pay tribute to all those who have pioneered the introduction of Portage into this country. Not just the professionals who realize its potential, but all those involved – district health authorities; social services departments; LEAs; supervisors and home visitors; voluntary associations who have cooperated by seconding staff for training as home visitors or who have offered funding, parents. We know that many have given freely of their own time and that many of the existing schemes could not survive without this. Let us also not forget the children themselves who have worked hard to make progress.

Education support grants: Portage-type projects

The government is pleased that the Local Authority Associations have also recognized the contribution of the Portage approach to the range of provision for children under five and that they have agreed to the inclusion of the establishment of Portage-type teams amongst the priority areas for support under the education support grant.

As many of you will be aware, grants will be available in 1986–87 to support expenditure totalling £1.2m for the provision by LEAs, in cooperation with other statutory and voluntary bodies, of multi-professional Portage-type teams to support parents in the education of children under five with special educational needs. Each scheme will be supported for three years and grants will be available over a five-year period. The grants will cover not just the establishment of entirely new teams, but also will be made to improve existing schemes where these do not conform to the guidelines of the National Portage Association. The support we have in mind here would, for example, cover the provision of clerical assistance or the establishment of proper management or supervisory structure where these do not exist. It would also cover the financing of home visitors where these are currently met from non-governmental sources.

Let me record here the government's thanks to the Executive of the National Portage Association for their cooperation in the development of this section. The preparation of the Guidelines for circulation to all LEAs, and their agreement to offer the necessary training for home visitors for authorities who are unable to mount their own courses is a valuable contribution. The one-day seminar, which took place only two days ago, for representatives from education, health and social services authorities who may be involved in mounting bids which the Executive volunteered to organize was also helpful. Without their support it is unlikely that the inclusion of Portage amongst the ESG priorities could have been made.

It is too early to say how many bids are likely to be received but the department has received numerous inquiries. The government hope to be able to support about 35 new teams in 1986–87 as well as providing assistance to up-rate a number of others. It is the aim that by the end of the five-year period for which support is planned, there will be at least one team in every LEA.

I am interested to learn that the theme of the Conference includes Extending and Developing Portage into schools.

The Portage approach may prove to have an important contribution to make to educational thinking in relation to children with special educational needs who attend schools and might, in turn, be enhanced by being school-based. Where school-based projects exist, there is evidence that they have resulted in both a reappraisal of the curriculum and its delivery and in attitudes towards, and ways of working with, parents of pupils of all ages. There is a much closer understanding of the needs of pupils generally which has strengthened parent/school contacts as well as having spin-off benefits for other children. In the context of pupils with special educational needs this bridging into school can lead to supported integration in a mainstream school where this is appropriate. A school-based multi-professional team in a special school is also in a position to offer a consistent continuum of support to a family of a statemented child from very early identification of need through to the years of schooling.

From the viewpoint of the team, a school-based project can offer a good support base and easier replacement of members who leave, since the school is normally in a position to command resources not readily available to other bases.

That said, however, perhaps a word of caution. Portage is essentially a home-based model of teaching for young children. Extension into schools therefore requires careful planning and coordination by staff. It may also require a commitment in resource terms which authorities might find hard to meet at the present time. It would be a pity if delivery of the service to parents of young children should suffer because some authorities involved felt that too rapid development along these lines was placing too many demands upon them.

Progress of implementation of 1981 Education Act

Portage is one of the encouraging features developing since the implementation of the 1981 Education Act. Much mud has been slung at the Act on the grounds that it is procedurally cumbersome and that it requires additional resources. In some respects this is true of the implementation of any major piece of social legislation. Inevitably it takes time to introduce and test procedures. Inevitably, too, the procedures have exposed gaps; notably the gap between the desirable and the possible; between the actual level of provision in some cases and the level required to meet reasonable need.

Narrowing these gaps necessitates careful planning. We must all recognize that the best is not always possible. Nor is it simply a question of the government providing additional resources. Until authorities have looked at ways of rationalizing their provision and have established effective methods of planning deployment of resources and have set up efficient methods of cooperation and liaison between services, the provision of additional resources from central government would be wasteful. It is to encourage this sort of joint programme that the government wishes to foster the introduction of Portage-type projects. The extension and development of the project into schools will encourage this joint planning to continue in relation to service delivery for older children.

There is never an ideal time to introduce new legislation. Progress will be slow initially but the Act has been generally welcomed and early evidence suggests that many children are now getting a better deal than previously.

The government is encouraged by the enormous strides that have been made since 1st April 1983:

- i Procedures are being implemented and they are speeding up. Many authorities are already reviewing their own procedures to streamline them and to improve communications with all concerned.
- ii The involvement of parents is also having positive effects. Parents themselves welcome the chance to contribute to assessments and reviews. This in turn promotes closer home/school links, whether in ordinary or special schools.
- iii Teachers are beginning to reassess their own approaches and curriculum delivery. This will also take time, particularly for teachers in mainstream schools. Integration requires forethought and training. In-service training for teachers in mainstream schools who have responsibility for children with special education needs remains a priority for special government funding.
- iv Closer cooperation is developing between health, social services and education authorities.
- v Many more children for whom special schools were never appropriate are now having their needs assessed. While many do not require the protection of a statement, many LEAs and schools are

now providing specialist help for them, for example, through peripatetic services available to all schools, or improved provision in school resulting in schools taking more responsibility for pupils with special needs.

vi Most authorities are reviewing their provision to meet special educational needs and are re-organizing their peripatetic services to provide more effective support. This applies not just to LEAs; in some areas speech therapists and other paramedical support services are also reviewing their organization and approaches to enable support to be spread over a greater number of schools where children have been integrated.

vii Progress towards integration is being made. But it cannot be rushed. It is better to move slowly but properly than to dash into ill-thought out placements.

We have made enormous strides in the last 2½ years. Inevitably progress has been too slow for some and too fast for others; too slow for the total integrationists; too fast for some teachers and schools. There is still a long way to go. But the Warnock Committee envisaged that implementation of its recommendations would take until the end of the century. Attitudes cannot be changed overnight and the first generation always has to fight the hardest battles.

It is difficult to get things right first time. The government prefers to see the Act as the basis from which progressive change can take place over time. Developments such as Portage are exciting and important and form part of these progressive changes. The scheme offers a constructive approach to parents who might well otherwise be isolated and helpless. The contribution which parents and the multi-professional teams make to the education service generally is one which the government welcomes and believes to be of value. I wish Portage and the National Portage Association well and I look forward to seeing its influence extend over the next five years.

Appendix: Extract from DES Draft Circular distributed to LEAs in England, June 1985

IX. THE PROVISION OF SERVICES TO SUPPORT PARENTS IN THE TEACHING OF CHILDREN UNDER FIVE, WITH SPECIAL EDUCATIONAL NEEDS

44 Grants will be available in 1986-1987 to support expenditure totalling up to £1.2m for the provision by LEAs in cooperation with other statutory and voluntary bodies, of multi-professional 'Portage' teams to support parents in the education of children under 5 years old who have special educational needs (SEN). Following the introduction of the Education Act 1981 LEAs are under a duty to make provision

for all children with SEN under the age of 5; although for those under 2 only with parental consent.

45 The Secretary of State wishes to encourage a scheme for promoting the development of children under five which employs a multi-professional approach. Portage schemes are particularly suitable because they are based on a teaching model and have proved highly effective in developing children with all forms of disability, including the most severe.

46 Each scheme accepted will be supported for not more than 3 years at a maximum expenditure of £28,000 per year. It is intended that new grants under this category should be available within the ESG programme over a period of 5 years. The Secretary of State hopes that this will enable every LEA to offer this service. Assistance with training and additional advice will also be available from the National Portage Association (Secretary, Mrs White, King Alfred's College, Sparkford Road, Winchester, Hants. Telephone Winchester 62281).

47 Applications should be submitted under one of the following headings:

- i the establishment of a new Portage team in authorities where no such service exists;
- ii the expansion of an existing service, or the improvement of a scheme which does not yet fulfil the criteria of the National Portage Association.

48 It is not anticipated that more than one bid will be accepted for each LEA in 1986-1987. The criteria for selection will include:

- i priority for providing an entirely new service;
- ii that the Authority demonstrates how the scheme relates to the criteria established by the National Portage Association in respect of management and supervisory structures, adequate clerical support and training of Portage workers;
- iii that the scheme does not aim to support more than 25 families initially;
- iv where bids are made in respect of expansion/improvement of existing service – that these either involve the establishment of additional teams where the size of the authority justifies it, or support for recently established teams which have hitherto not attracted secure funding from authority sources.

49 All bids for support for Portage Schemes will have to certify that the proposals are not currently funded from other Government sources (eg under the Urban Programme).

50 For all approved schemes LEAs will be required to provide an annual report to be submitted by 31 July each year. This should set out details of the establishment of the scheme and the training of staff, the numbers of children supported and a brief report on each child's progress. A brief initial report will be required from any authority claiming an allocation for the first time in the period 1 April – 31 July in any year.

Portage in Different Settings in Northamptonshire

Christine Dickinson and Barbara McDowell

Background details

In 1983 the educational facilities for the under-fives in Northamptonshire included education nurseries and special schools, social services nurseries and two peripatetic teachers for the pre-school handicapped (PTPH).

Portage materials have been used by the pre-school teachers since January 1982 and also in a special school as its curriculum base.

The impetus to set up a traditional Portage home teaching project occurred when a new educational psychologist was appointed, who had already supervised a Portage home teaching service. By working together with another Portage-trained educational psychologist, a team with sufficient force to promote the development of Portage in the county was formed.

During the next two years interest in Portage within the county escalated. This was probably a product of the increased publicity and activities related to the pilot home teaching project. These included a termly Portage newsletter and talks to interested groups by Portage supervisors and invited speakers.

Meetings of the Midlands National Portage Association have also been held in the county. This interest led to many requests for Portage training and the consequent adaptation of the Portage model for use in a variety of settings. The proliferation in the use of Portage has been the result of training people on a Portage workshop.

Three-day Portage workshop

The present workshop is the result of many adaptations which have been made as the perceived needs of the participants have changed. It consists of a basic core of modules with materials which can be selected according to whether participants will be using the Portage model in a home-teaching or in a day-base situation in a school, nursery, hospital or hostel.

The workshop consists of short lectures using videos and slides followed by individual, partner or small group practical work. The emphasis is upon using the practical sessions to provide concrete ways of enabling the participants to learn and practise using the skills being taught.

The workshop is designed to provide information and teach skills under the following headings:

(i) What is Portage?
  - home teaching and day-base models
  - support and monitoring system
  - case studies

(ii) Where did it come from?
  - short history of its development and spread

(iii) What happens during a Portage home visit or Portage teaching sessions?

(iv) What materials are used?
  - Portage checklists and cards
  - alternative checklists and teaching materials
  - materials for language development

(v) How to teach new skills:
  - identifying behaviours to teach
  - what influences behaviour
  - how to set short- and long-term teaching targets
  - how to make it enjoyable for the child
  - what can we manipulate to maximize the chances of success

(vi) How to write activity charts

(vii) How to deal with difficult behaviour

(viii) How to ensure what's learnt isn't soon forgotten

(ix) Portage and play

(x) Use of the Portage model in schools and nurseries

(xi) Developing links with other professionals

(xii) What makes the positive Portage system

(xiii) The National Portage Association.

The use of the Portage model in each of the settings is described.

Pilot home teaching project

This is a classic Portage home teaching service.

Following extensive communications during 1983 with health, social services and education departments through meetings, written papers, letters and a very successful introductory talk by R.J. Cameron it was agreed that a small pilot project be set up.

Home teachers from a variety of backgrounds were trained and two teams formed from personnel from the social services and education departments. These teams have worked with a total of 16 families during a 12-month pilot period.

Home teachers are released from their existing duties to visit their family(s) and attend a fortnightly staff meeting. There have been two voluntary workers participating in the project at different times. Each team is jointly supervised by one of the authors and a pre-school teacher. The management team consists of senior officers from education and social services who meet bi-monthly.

The project is unfunded apart from travelling expenses and a small lump sum for toys and materials.

The project has been fully evaluated. The information collected from the home teachers and parents involved was extremely positive. All the children involved achieved a very high percentage of the activities set.

Several of the home teachers stated that they had found it difficult to 'do justice' to their Portage work since it was in addition to their full-time existing responsibilities. There were also comments regarding the necessary goodwill of colleagues covering for their absences when completing Portage work.

Portage in a nursery setting

Nursery nurses and teachers (education), officers and assistants (social services) who attended the adapted Portage workshop have utilized the materials and techniques in a variety of ways. Just one example is cited here – a social services day nursery where all the nursery staff are Portage trained.

A large proportion of the day nursery children have special needs. Referrals to the nursery are made by health visitors, social workers, educational psychologists and the local child development centre. The children are carefully monitored and reviewed every three months. There is a ratio of two adults to nine children in each of the six classrooms and an officer-in-charge and a deputy officer (the latter being a member of the Northampton Portage home teaching team).

Portage checklists or alternative developmental checklists are completed (in consultation with parent(s)) for children about whom there is concern. Long-term objectives are then planned with possible reference to visiting professionals, e.g. educational psychologist, speech therapist, etc. Short-term objectives are then set by the nursery officers who may consult with other nursery staff for support and ideas where necessary. An example of a completed activity chart is provided (Figure 1). Although some activities are taught on a one-to-one basis with every trial recorded, many are built into group and play situations.

Portage is therefore used in the nursery in the following ways:

(i) One-to-One daily teaching – which is charted as in 'classic' model.
(ii) Group activity – previously taught activities are practised in group situations (generalization).
(iii) Group activity – a new teaching task is set for each child in the group. This is a direct teaching situation where different children will be asked to do different tasks.

Figure 1: Example of a completed activity chart

PORTAGE ACTIVITY CHART: (SCHOOL/NURSERY USE)

NAME OF SCHOOL/NURSERY F.N.
CHILD'S NAME: S.C. DATE OF BIRTH:
CHILD'S TEACHER(S): N.T.
WEEK BEGINNING: 26.8.85

TEACHING TARGETS FOR WEEK

1 *General objectives for the week – for maintenance, generalization and practice (including note of materials to use and general instructions):*

(a) Play – limited choice: peg board, posting boxes, form boards – if chosen N.T. joins in using 'prompts' as appropriate.

(b) Snack time – S.C. to use Makaton sign for drink, biscuit, please and thank you (gestural or physical prompts).

(c) Group activity – S.C. to follow one element instruction using Makaton signs. (Other children following 2/3/4 element instructions as appropriate using prepositions.)

Comments on the above by the end of the week:

(a) Chose post box and smiled while completing.
(b) Likes food! Signed for drink and biscuit.
(c) Selected book needed gestural prompts to sign.

Home-teaching suggestions:
S.C. to sign for her book at bedtime.

2 *Specific teaching activity for daily teaching and recording (including : teaching instructions, materials to use, correction procedure, rewards, place to work, etc.):*

Teaching objective = S.C. will go to toilet on request, wash and dry her hands. (Child had already mastered in previous weeks, using the toilet independently.)

Directions =

At hourly intervals say 'go toilet' and use sign. Give prompts as required, praise at each stage, then allow her to choose classroom activity.

Record each visit: √ = independent
V = verbal prompt
G = gestural prompt
P = physical prompt

CRIT.=6/7

TOILET TIMES	MON	TUES	WED	THUR	FRI
3 pm	V	G	V	V	√
2	V/P	V	P	P	V
1	V	V	V	V	√
12	V	V	√	√	√
11	V/G	V/G	√	√	√
10	P/G	P/V/G	V	√	√
9 am	P/G	P/G	V	V	V

OUTCOME: Success ☐ Continued ☐ Changed ☑ Abandoned ☐

(iv) Play – but with limited choices of toys/activities (linked to the teaching objectives for each child) placed within the room on set occasions.

Children who do not work well in a one-to-one situation have particularly benefited from the flexibility of this approach. They can be placed on a structured programme which is presented within group and play situations.

The use of Portage in the nursery has resulted in an increase in the amount of teaching each child receives. There has also been a noticable improvement in the prevention and management of behaviour problems.

Parents who wish to be involved with their children's programmes visit the nursery and are given details of activities to practise at home.

Portage in a school setting

Teachers from special and mainstream schools and nurseries have attended the modified Portage workshops. Their use of Portage varies according to their place of work, the number of children with identified special needs, the involvement of other teachers, and the level of parental involvement. Two examples are described; in each case the teachers involved are special needs coordinators (SNC). SNC have been appointed within all Northamptonshire mainstream schools to act as liaison teachers for children with special needs, their parents, teachers and support services. They all coordinate the 1981 Education Act procedures within their school.

1. A Portage trained teacher uses the Portage model in her role as special needs coordinator in a lower school. She works with colleagues setting up and monitoring individual teaching programmes for children with identified special needs.

The stages of the process are outlined in the flow chart below:

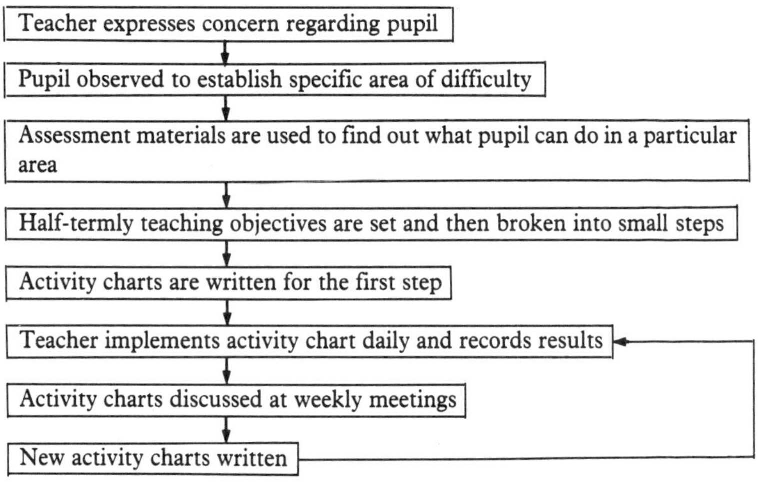

The school uses a range of observation techniques. The assessment materials used include ELSA skills lists (Ainscow and Tweddle, 1984) written by the teachers which may or may not be derived from curriculum material.

At present the scheme is only operating with two teachers and a very small number of children.

There are plans to extend and modify the scheme to involve more teachers. At present parents are informed but not involved.

It is interesting to note that the teachers have commented on spin-off benefits which affect the child's behaviour or performance in an area quite different to that included in the charting; for example, an increase in confidence, which resulted in the child talking more to adults and children when the charted activity involved pencil skills.

2. Similarly another special needs coordinator for a lower school uses her Portage training in her role as SNC. She works with other reception class teachers to set half-termly objectives for children causing concern. These are discussed at regular meetings with the school's educational psychologist (one of the authors). The parents are then invited into school to ask if they would like to participate in the programme by working on set activities at home. To date all parents have agreed and a home-school book has been started for each child. The teacher writes instructions for teaching each activity in the home-school books. The teacher sometimes models the activity for the parents and may also supply the materials. The parents record comments on the child's performance on the tasks set and these are discussed during a weekly visit to school. The parents involved have commented that they welcome this increased involvement in their child's education, and on the whole the children have achieved the tasks set.

It is now felt that this method of working will be helpful for older children in the school but using school-based curriculum materials.

Portage in a hospital setting

Several medical therapists from the child development centre (CDC) based at a local hospital have attended Portage workshops. The teacher based at the CDC is a member of the home teaching project.

The *medical therapists* are using Portage with children as a follow-up to assessment in the following ways:

i) to set activities directly for their own use or as part of the treatment given by a treatment nurse during the hospital visit.
ii) to set activities during the weekly hospital visit which the parents can then do at home on a daily basis with their child.

Figure 2: Portage service to a child and the support network

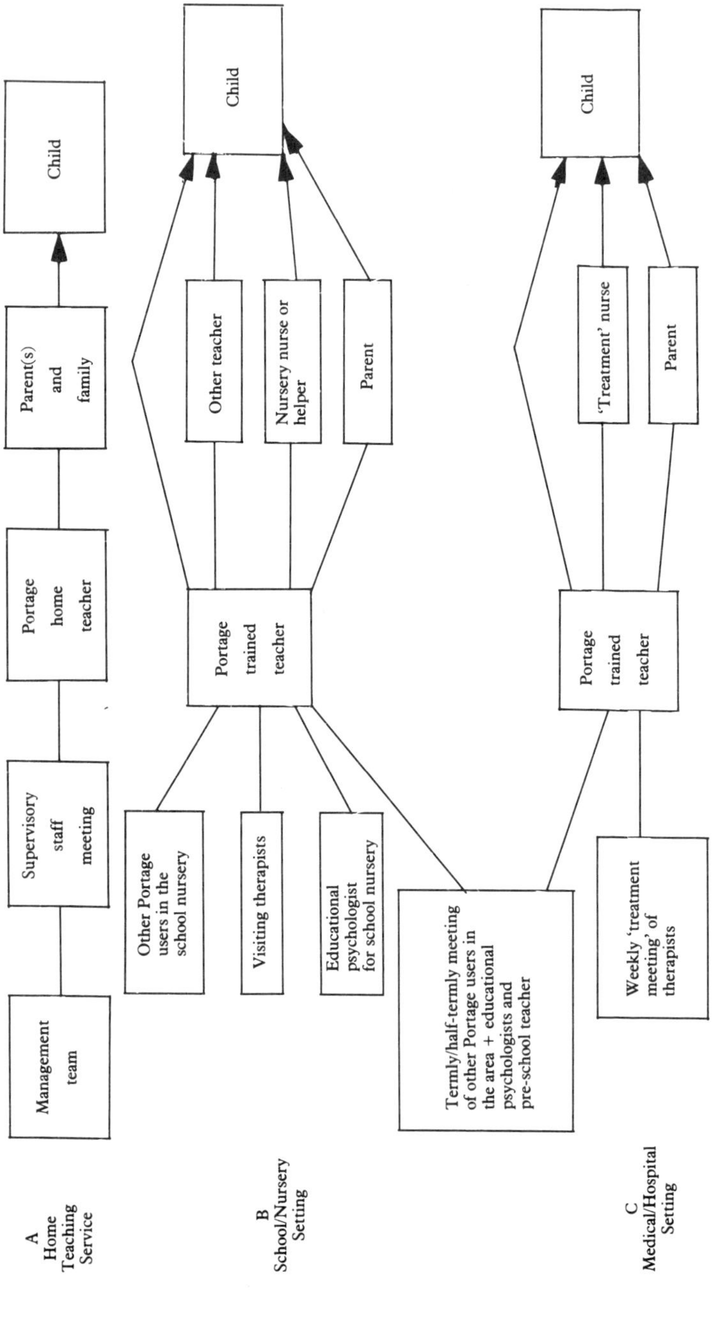

The *teacher* based at the CDC also sets activities for parents to complete with their children at home. This is completed during either home or hospital visits.

Support systems and service delivery

Although all the uses of Portage described above vary according to the client group and work setting, in each case there is a support network. This is illustrated in Figure 2 which clearly shows the similarities in the service delivery, support and monitoring networks.

One noticable difference from the classic home teaching model in some of the examples cited is that the individual following the agreed activities with the child is a highly trained professional. In this situation it may be that the amount of detail specified on certain sections of the chart may be reduced. The place of work, use of prompts, correction procedure, etc., will be agreed but not recorded in detail for each weekly teaching step.

Summary and conclusions

The Portage model in Northamptonshire has developed rapidly during the last two years. It has been adapted for use in a wide number of settings. These include homebase, school, nursery and hospital.

In each of the settings regardless of adaptation the following components are adhered to:

1 Clear teaching targets are set
2 Teaching targets and the results of teaching are recorded
3 A support and monitoring system is built in.

Future

We hope to be able to continue to adapt and improve our workshops to enable participants to gain information and skills which they will be able to use in their own working environments.

We also hope that use of education support grant funds will enable the continuation and extension of the home teaching service in the county.

Editors' note: Christine Dickinson and Barbara McDowell's chapter presents a neat description of Portage in a variety of settings in Northamptonshire. Their chapter aptly fits the theme of the book: 'extending and developing Portage.'

The settings include a home-based service, a nursery school, a mainstream lower school and a hospital and though the approach is modified to cater for the variety, the authors emphasize that in each case there is a supportive network and appropriate training is given, clear training targets are set and the results of teaching are recorded. These are all important aspects of the Portage service delivery model.

Portage in Perspective: Parental Involvement in Pre-school Programmes

Gillian Pugh

Looking back at the papers from the last three Portage Conferences, it is hard to know what there is left to add, since they cover every conceivable aspect of the growth and development of Portage throughout Britain. I certainly won't presume to write anything new about Portage, but what perhaps I can do, as an 'outsider', is to put Portage into a wider perspective, and to look at where it fits in the burgeoning field of parental involvement in pre-school programmes.

I first became familiar with Portage in 1980 when I included descriptions of three schemes in a small book I was writing on intervention schemes and group work with families of handicapped children (Pugh, 1981). At that time most people still thought it was some fancy French idea, and even in the special education field there were few who understood its potential. Since then I have been involved in two pieces of work upon which I shall draw: a national study of preparation, eduction and support for parents published in 1984 as *The Needs of Parents* (Pugh and De'Ath, 1984), which included incidentally a special study of pre-school home visiting schemes (published separately (Aplin and Pugh, 1983)): and a current study of parent-professional relationships in pre-school services. This is a national study funded by DHSS, and is looking at parental involvement right across the board – in health services, education and social services and the voluntary sector.

Why parental involvement?

The terms 'parental involvement, 'parent-professional partnership' and 'parents as educators' have become fashionable in recent years, and tend to be thrown about with little regard to their true meaning. Many of those who work in health, education and social services are being urged to work more closely with parents, and looking at how services have developed it is indeed illogical to imagine that schools should feel they can educate, or hospitals cure, children without the close collaboration of those children's parents.

Yet if we look at the reasons given for working more closely with parents, these tend to vary depending on whether the benefits are seen to accrue to the child, the parents or the professionals. As far as children's educational development is concerned, the research, from the 1960s onwards, has confirmed the crucial role that parents play in their children's development. In Britain we have been particularly influenced by the American Headstart programmes which showed (despite a few hiccups early on) that early intervention programmes for socially disadvantaged children, which involved parents, had a greater long-term effect than those which did not (Bronfenbrenner, 1974). The view that the family is the most effective system for fostering and sustaining the long-term development of children, lay behind parallel developments in behavioural programmes for handicapped children. These simple truths have influenced the thinking behind most of the major government reports concerned with children in the last 25 years (Plowden, Bullock, Court ('we have found no better way to raise a child than to reinforce the ability of his parents to do so'), Taylor and Warnock).

The logical extension of this growing view of parents as educators of their children has been to devise programmes which have attempted to sustain parents in their educational role, through a variety of educational home visiting schemes attached to schools, home-based intervention schemes (such as Portage) and parent education programmes. I will return to some of these later. At a more general level, research such as that by Tizard and Hughes (1984) confirmed what most of us knew anyway – that without any special programmes at all, young children learn more from talking to their parents than ever they do from talking to busy nursery teachers.

These developments have stressed the benefit to the children, but there is also a growing recognition that parents too may benefit from a closer working relationship with pre-school workers, and a greater involvement in planning and determining services. Evidence from our study of the needs of parents showed that parents tended to feel confused and lacking in confidence in the face of professional expertise. They were aware of the crucial partt they played in the early years of their children's lives, and were made to feel that there must be a 'right' way to bring children up if only they could work out which expert to believe. This was particularly acute for parents of children with special needs who wanted help in teaching their children to do things that others did naturally, leading some (as Cunningham and Sloper's earlier study (1978) had shown) to feel very isolated from their child. 'They also think they should not try what they intuitively feel is right, unless an "expert" has advised it. The result is non-activity and usually slower development in the infant.'

Our own work led us to believe that if parents were enabled to contribute to as well as receive services, thus building on their skills and developing their self-confidence, this would provide a firmer base for a more equal relationship between them and professional workers. Many parents in this country, of course, do set up and run their own groups – playgroups, opportunity groups, parent and toddler groups, community nurseries. These have not only given parents greatly increased insight into how children grow, behave and develop, but also the skills and confidence of working in the community.

The other development from the parents' point of view is the move towards making services more accountable to those who pay for them through taxes and rates. Although we are still a long way behind some of our European and American colleagues, the 1980 and 1981 Education Acts have opened the door to parents. Greater availability of information, choice of school, and the inclusion of parents on school governing bodies (at present still something of a token gesture) are an important start. Potentially the 1981 Act has more far-reaching implications, if the rights it affords to parents – to be involved in assessment procedures and in decisions regarding placement – are extended to all parents.

From the professional's point of view a closer relationship with parents offers opportunities for overcoming some of the many discontinuities between home and school. Whether the professional is working with a child with a particular problem or developmental delay, or running a pre-school group, the experience will be of greatest value if it relates to what happens at home and can complement it. There is also the hope that services will be able to respond more directly to need; that problems can be shared and more accurately identified; and that a greater trust can be created.

The extent of parental involvement

It is of course quite impossible to gauge the exact extent to which parents and professionals are working together, but my feeling is that despite the recommendations of countless government reports, parental involvement is not as widespread as it might be. It does however depend on how it is defined, as I shall show shortly. The recent report from the Child Health and Education Study (Osborn, 1984), based on 13,000 children, makes disappointing reading. Contrary to popular opinion less than half of the mothers with children at playgroups had helped in the group during the previous term and only a quarter helped once a month. In LEA nursery schools, only 13 per cent helped once a term, whilst day nurseries found difficulty in generating any kind of parental or community activities.

As far as home visiting is concerned, as cuts begin to bite eductional home visiting schemes appear to be dwindling, although an increasing number of teachers are visiting homes as part of their work in nursery and infant schools. The main growth points seem to be Portage (which I gather now has 150 schemes) and Homestart, the scheme which trains parents as home visitors and is now in 50 different locations.

In our own inquiry we asked all local authorities and health authorities to what extent services for families with children under five were planned, implemented and delivered in partnership with those for whom they were intended. Very few of those who replied could point to any examples, though there were many references to involvement. Interestingly, a surprising number assumed that we must only be interested in children with special needs and told us of Portage and similar schemes.

In concluding her study of parental involvement in nursery and infant schools, Tizard *et al.* (1981) suggested that 'there is a discrepancy between the approval in principle of parent involvement in early eduction and the extent to which it is realised in practice.... The most enthusiastic advocates seem to be furthest from the coal face.' My feeling is that there is a lot of support and interest at the coal face, but that unless it can be married to support from middle and top management, so that resources and training are made available, there will be very little further progress.

Parental involvement or partnership?

Despite the increasing commitment on the part of many pre-school workers to involve parents more fully in the services they provide, the tendency is still for professionals to invite parents to join them on *their* terms. Yet a true partnership suggests an acceptance of equal skills and experience, and a sense that each partner brings something different but of equal value to the relationship.

The tendency to treat parents as deficient in some way, and in need of treatment or advice, has perhaps obscured the fact that most parents are well able to contribute to as well as receive services. As the Warnock Report recognized, 'Parents can be effective partners only if professionals take notice of what they say and how they express their needs, and treat their contributions as intrinsically important'.

Speaking at a study day at the National Children's Bureau, Hilton Davis put it like this:

> Partnership is a relationship in which the professional services the parents, by making appropriate expertise available to them for their consideration. The relationship is, therefore, one of *complementary expertise*, since the expert knowledge of the parents, on themselves, their aims, their situation generally, and their children, complements what the profession has to offer including professional knowledge and the skills to communicate it. Using this framework of partnership therefore, the professional accepts his/her expertise and limitations; perceives parents as knowledgeable; acknowledges that many of the problems are not easily resolved; and believes that the best approach is to pool their expertise and to experiment together in mutually agreed ways. Although the parents are seen as having ultimate executive control, the professional's role is to offer for discussion alternative ways of viewing the situation and intervening. Decisions, therefore, are made on the basis of negotiation. (Davis, 1985)

Dimensions of parental involvement

In order to put parental involvement and partnership into context, I would like to show briefly a typology that we have devised to illustrate the various dimensions of parent involvement. This is based on work we have done in more than 100 pre-school schemes and centres, and on research done by others in this field. It should not be seen as a progression from one end of the spectrum to the other, but simply as a way of describing the different ways in which parents relate to pre-school services.

1 Non-participation

In some schemes, particularly those providing substitute care for children of working parents, parents are unlikely to be involved on a daily basis (although they may be involved in management). But there are also many parents who do not participate for other reasons – because they lack confidence, are tired or depressed, or feel that a language barrier presents too many problems, or because they do not understand the value or relevance of what is on offer (for example, a language stimulation programme).

2 External support

This is perhaps most relevant to groups and schemes which parents may support from the outside, without actually becoming involved. For example, through fund raising, attending social functions, offering moral support when services are threatened by cuts, etc.

3 Participation

There are many ways in which parents can participate in pre-school services, under the supervision of professional staff. They can provide an 'extra pair of hands' for busy nursery teachers, either by working with small groups of children or by servicing the group – mending toys, making tea, washing paint pots. Parents can be asked to welcome other parents to the group; they may enjoy sharing in their own children's learning; they may be able to run a toy library or mother and toddler group. Parents may also be able to participate in observation and assessment of their child; attend review panels; or enjoy nominal participation in users' committees or governing bodies.

4 Partnership

Partnership suggests a sharing of power, resources, knowledge and decision-making between parents and professionals. It can be seen in three different ways.

(a) *Partnership between an individual parent and a professional*. This is the kind of partnership to which Hilton Davis was referring, and it suggests mutual respect, a sharing of different but equivalent expertise, and a sharing of information. Portage offers an ideal framework for developing skills in assessment, in writing reports, in evaluating the effectiveness of services, in negotiating appropriate placements and in working their way round the system. It gives them the tools and the confidence to 'take on' professionals, and it offers professionals the tools for working with parents on a more equal footing.

But if parents are really to be able to negotiate they are also going to have to understand professional jargon and find a way of communicating their own views. The 'parent profile' that Sheila Wolfendale has been developing provides a simple format for parents to use in describing their child at home, under appropriate developmental headings. The information can then be used as a basis for dialogue, to explore different perceptions and aspirations between parent and professional for a given child (Wolfendale, 1985).

(b) *Partnership between parents in general and a particular group or scheme.* If parents are to be partners in running a service, this implies an equal sharing of power over resources, over knowledge and information, and over decision making. Although there is some parent involvement in management of schools, and parents are often on the management committees of Portage projects, whether or not this can be defined as partnership depends very much on whether anyone listens to what they have to say. My feeling from talking to a number of parents of children with special needs is that often their problems are such that they are happier to leave the management to someone else.

Partnership is also implicit in the growing number of schemes in which parents are taking on roles as workers – visiting homes (for example the 50 or so Homestart schemes, some Portage schemes, or the parents who are home-school liaison workers in Coventry); offering counselling and support to parents of newly diagnosed handicapped infants (the Southend scheme, and Kids in Camden); convening groups (Scope in Southampton, or the Riverside Health Project in Newcastle); or setting up and running toy libraries and parent and toddler groups.

(c) *Partnership between parents/clients/consumers and policy makers.* This is still all too rare, but is perhaps best illustrated by the important part parents play in Strathclyde's link up groups; and by the growing involvement of parents in community health councils, under-fives committees, district handicap teams, patients participation groups in general practice, neighbourhood health projects and occasionally district health authorities and local council committees.

5 Control

These would be services in which parents both determine and implement decisions, and are ultimately responsible and accountable. For example, community playgroups, parent and toddler groups and community nurseries.

These groupings should not be seen as progressive, and in any one centre or service different parents will relate in different ways, but they have helped us to distinguish between how professionals think they are relating to parents, and what is actually happening.

Home-based services: some advantages and disadvantages

I would now like to put Portage into the context of some other home-based schemes, and consider briefly some advantages and disadvantages of an approach which theoretically offers considerable opportunities for partnership.

The survey of home visiting schemes undertaken by the National Children's Bureau (Aplin and Pugh, 1983) revealed a marked shift from the earlier emphasis placed on children's cognitive and social performance, towards a focus on supporting families in the vital role they play in children's overall development. Schemes were obviously very different depending on whether they were based on schools, or were funded by adult education, or were run by voluntary organizations – but the general feeling was that the work is most effective when it is directed as much to the parents as to the children. Perhaps the three aims of the Inner London schemes can best illustrate this:

(a) to develop the parent/child relationship;
(b) to encourage the personal growth of the parent;
(c) to develop effective links between the family and the wider community.

So perhaps in contrast to Portage, most home visiting schemes have become less directly educational and highly structured, and more generally supportive to the family as a whole.

Some advantages

1 The service offered can respond directly to the parents' needs, and parents can select priorities.

2 A working partnership is inevitable, if goals are planned together and assessed together.

3 Parents can be helped to develop skills in a way that does not undermine their self-confidence. It can confirm that parents are doing alright, as this London mother says 'It's really good having someone to talk to – someone who listens to you. Lots of the time you were doing the right thing for the children, but talking it over makes you feel more sure' (Aplin and Pugh,

1983). It provides also some structure when there are particular problems: 'We can do a certain amount by instinct, but you reach a stage when you need more' (mother at Kids).

The evidence on the effectiveness of home visiting schemes is in fact rather more compelling for the parents than it is for children, showing improved morale, and a greater understanding of and interest in their children (e.g. McCail, 1981, Burden, 1980).

4 Schemes can provide a basis for developing skills in assessment, joint planning and in decision making.

5 Many schemes are able to forge closer links between home and school, not only helping parents to understand what teachers are trying to do with their children, but also giving teachers an insight into the homes and families of the children they teach.

6 The programme and the level of involvement can be matched to other demands and commitments within the family and other family members can be involved.

7 Programmes can deal with problems where they occur, and behaviour can be learned in context. There is a greater chance of long-term gain if the programmes are based on existing skills and are restructuring what is already happening.

8 Home visitors can reach out to parents who may not seek help. Shinman's study (1981) showed that even if there were clinics and playgroups on every corner of every street, depression, alienation and lack of confidence would prevent up to a quarter of all mothers from using them.

9 Home visitors may also be able to help to establish community networks. A study of Homestart (van der Eyken, 1982) found that those who were not coping either did not have or were unable to use social networks. The home visitors were able to help families reach the point where, for the first time, they could use networks and cope adequately on their own.

Disadvantages/limitations

No approach is without its limitations, and I would like to remind you briefly what some of these are.

1 An intensive home visiting programme can put intolerable pressures on some families.

2 One of the myths that Tony Dessent exploded was that anyone can visit homes. Home-based programmes are only as good as the home visitor, and working in people's homes is a skilled and difficult task.

3 If parents are made to feel responsible for their children's success as they acquire new skills, so too will they feel they must take responsibility for failures. As previous Portage conferences have recognized, there is danger in a cook-book approach based on recipes rather than principles. And there is danger too in using the child's performance to measure the parent's success.

4 Unless home-based schemes involve fathers as well as mothers, they can become divisive, giving one parent skills and techniques that are not shared.

5 Home is not always ideal. Cold floors for physiotherapy or the constant accompaniment of the television when a language programme is in progress can be frustrating. As Sandow and Clarke (1978) reminded us: 'The home may be so elegant and the mother so concerned with its effect on the visitor, that the purpose of the visit becomes obscured. Alternatively one may be required to work in a room ten feet by eight, surrounded by three generations of a mutually hostile family, in an atmosphere composed of equal parts smoke, sweat and old chip papers'.

6 And finally, home-based programmes do not solve problems of loneliness and isolation, nor do they give an exhausted parent any time off.

Issues and dilemmas

The various points I have made raise a number of issues and point to some unresolved dilemmas.

1 Are we able to start from where parents are at, rather than where we would like them to be? Can we recognize that unless parents' own problems are resolved, then to present a structured programme that depends on their involvement and commitment may increase feelings of quilt and anxiety. Two years ago, Jo Cameron spoke of her needs as a parent for counselling and support, and suggested that there are times when the needs of the rest of the family, or of the parent must take precedence. This is supported by the experience at Honeylands, for example (Burden, 1980) and by many of the educational home visiting schemes, which stress the need to work through family problems before focusing on the child. The Inner London scheme for example analysed the content of 200 home visits and found that 200 out of 500 topics that came up during visits were to do with problems of health or marital relationships or housing and were beyond the original aims of the scheme (Aplin and Pugh, 1983).

2 We need to be conscious of the dangers of 'professionalizing' parenthood, and of increasing parents' guilt and anxiety by over-emphasizing the need for their commitment to a home-based programme. Partnership suggests discussion and negotiation and the possibility of saying 'No, I can't cope with any more at the moment'.

3 Is partnership possible when professional values are the ones that are operational? Most parental involvement is dictated on professionals' terms – 'you help us in the ways we think fit, and we will help you bring up your children better'. But even in schemes which affect a partnership, there are difficulties. I have been able to observe many home visitors at work – as part of Portage schemes, or the health visitors working with the child development project, or educational home visitors working with the child development project, or educational home visitors. I am constantly struck by the

conflict between the need to give guidance and enforce a structure, and the wish to respond to the parents' needs. Sarah Sandow summed it up well at the 1982 Conference when she was discussing the mutual selection of objectives: 'care must be taken that this does not mean careful massaging of parental ambitions to fit the tutor's own view of the case. If the parent is to have true power, she must have more than the right to admiringly agree to the tutor's suggestions. But can the professional take a back seat if the selection of objectives seems inappropriate or even perverse?'

I feel that this issue presents very real problems, that are far from being resolved.

4 Our study of the needs of parents revealed the importance of flexibility and of having a range of services in a community that might give parents some choice. The needs of individual families obviously vary enormously and will change over a period of time, and whilst Portage is clearly meeting a very real need, it may not be the perfect answer to every parents' problems. As Sue Buckley reminded us, again at the 1982 Conference, there is still no adequate evidence on the comparative value of home-based and centre-based services, and as I have shown there are some inadequacies in a purely home-based scheme. I have been doing some work in the Kids centre in Camden, where the home learning scheme is linked both to developmental play sessions where five or six children and their parents come together on a weekly basis in the centre; and to individual counselling and support from the centre staff. The parents seem to appreciate this combination of individual work in the home, and the experience of a group.

5 Appropriate training is another key issue. I have already referred to the essential qualities required for home visiting. The first home visiting scheme in Britain (in the West Riding of Yorkshire as part of the EPA project in Denaby) describes a home visitor as needing to be 'unbiased, non-judgemental, able to work under any conditions, knowledgeable without being dictatorial, helpful without being partronising, able to listen, and sensitive to people's needs without appearing into their private affairs' (Smith, 1975).

These qualities could equally refer to anyone working with parents, and yet our study of parent education programmes (Pugh and De'Ath, 1984) concluded that the training of most pre-school workers seemed to pay little attention to developing skills in listening, in self-awareness, in understanding and accepting values different from one's own, and in expressing ideas in language that is not riddled with jargon.

If we are asking professionals to work with parents as partners, to listen to what they say, to be prepared to negotiate and discuss and plan together, and occasionally to admit to not knowing the answer – then this does, I suggest, have considerable implications for initial and in-service training.

6 In our experience, a more open relationship with parents reflects a greater sharing and participation (a) between members of staff in a team or a unit; and (b) between the many professionals who are working with families in a neighbourhood.

7 And finally, to conclude on a note of caution, I think we should ask whether the current emphasis on parental involvement always implies a more open relationship and shared care, or whether sometimes responsibility for children's welfare and education is being shifted from professionals to parents and self-help groups. It is important that at this time of cutbacks and economic recession we look at the rationale for parent-professional partnership. Some, for example are seeing parents in classrooms and hospitals as cheap labour, releasing teachers to do 'proper' teaching and nurses to do the 'real' caring. Similarly, in promoting self-help and community activities are we simply supporting a cut-back in expenditure on state support for families? These are important questions that need answering. Participation of parents can just be a way of passing problems back to those parents.

In conclusion

In principle, we can I think justify the concept of partnership between parents and professionals, for the long-term benefits it brings to the children; for the increased self-esteem and self-confidence and knowledge it brings to parents; and for the opportunities it offers professionals to respond more directly to need and provide a service based on mutual trust and respect.

In practice, I would suggest it is a great deal more difficult. It requires appropriate attitudes and skills, sufficient time and resources, and a willingness on the part of both parents and professionals to share – information, decision making and mutual respect. But ultimately it is a question of overall philosophy – do we really believe in working *with* parents to meet their needs, rather than always doing things to them?

My feeling is that Portage provides the right framework for taking this partnership forward, and that you could with advantage spread your ideas and approaches beyond the world of special education.

Editors' note: Gillian Pugh's justification for the notion of partnership between parents and professionals is explained. The importance of the partnership between home visitor and parent is that each brings something of equal value to that partnership – the home visitor may have the professional skills of task analysis, goal setting, etc., but the parent brings his or her knowledge of the child and all that this entails. This combining of expertise, knowledge and skills creates the partnership which forms the basis for a successful Portage project. If Portage provides the right framework for establishing this relationship, then this relationship could be continued when the child starts school. Gillian Pugh concludes that Portage does provide the right framework for taking this partnership further into the future.

An Intervention Package to Teach Parents, Residential Care Staff and Teachers of Children and Adults with Severe Learning Difficulties and Seriously Self-defeating Behaviours

Albert Kushlick, Jane Hubert and John Smith

Results from an epidemiological survey of urban and rural areas in southern England have shown that in a population of 100,000 there are approximately 100 children and 130 adults with severe learning difficulties. Of these, roughly 80 per cent of children, and 40 per cent of adults, are living at home with their parents (Kushlick and Cox, 1973).

Among the numbers of people with severe learning difficulties are some 10 children and 16 adults who have severely disruptive behaviours, i.e. they are self-injurious, aggressive to others, damage the environment, are noisy, non-compliant or generally disruptive. A proportion are very lacking in self-help skills including incontinence and, probably because of the presence of some or many of these behaviour problems, only half of these children live at home with their parents, and an even smaller proportion (12 per cent) of adults with similar problems are still living at home, presumably because with current methods of management, as the children grow larger and stronger, it becomes even more difficult to manage them in a 'normal' environment – i.e. one designed for people with a wide range of social and intellectual skills. Many parents want to keep their child at home, but find it not only frustrating but also very stressful. Routine activities such as eating, dressing, bathing and toileting take much longer than is expected in a 'normal' person of equivalent age, because of the very disruptive behaviour and general non-compliance. Without special skills, caring adults provide little or no opportunity for these people to learn new relevant skills, and they have a tendency to arrange routine activities in a way which avoids immediate trouble either by placating and giving in to the demands of the person with severe learning difficulties or by reacting angrily to them, rather than attempting, despite the person's resistance and tantrums, calmly to prompt or correct directed tasks and celebrate their successes.

At present there are only four specialist units in England which specifically confront these very challenging behaviours and teach the people involved new appropriate skills. They are, for children, Hilda Lewis House, run by the National Health Service, Beech Tree House (North and South) run by the Spastics Society and, for adults, St. Andrews, a private hospital in

Northampton. These units obviously cannot serve all the relevant families throughout the country and of the few whose children can enter one of these, only parents living nearby can continue to take part routinely and systematically in the lives of their children while they are there, and when they leave, so that they can apply the procedures confidently when the children are at home. Teachers or residential workers from the children's home cannot at present participate in these programmes.

At the moment, therefore, when these people are perceived as 'too difficult' to be managed by their parents, by the teachers in special schools, by instructors in social education centres, and residential care staff in short-term and respite care units, they may be transferred to the long-stay wards of traditional hospitals. There is evidence that in these hospitals the mortality rates of people with challenging behaviours are higher than average (Kushlick and Cox, 1973), partly through self-injury and the ingestion of inedible objects (Foxx and Livesay, 1984) and partly through the use of tranquillizers which, in high dosages, reduce the cough reflex and thus contribute to death from respiratory infections. It is significant, too, that in inquiries into allegations of ill-treatment in hospitals for people called mentally handicapped, those with very challenging behaviours are frequently involved (DHSS, 1969 and 1978). The problems presented by the management of people with such challenging, disruptive, self-injurious, self-stimulating and aggressive behaviours have been discussed in the Jay Report (DHSS, 1979) and in a special report of a DHSS study team (DHSS, 1984) and there has been much discussion on the redesigning and restaffing of residential units. Ideological commitments have been made by the government (DHSS, 1980) to generate high quality care, but little experimental or procedural work has been directed towards developing creative, interesting and educational programmes that are effective in the presence of very disruptive behaviours occurring within residential units, schools or at home.

The need for effective and replicable procedures is undeniable, and recent evidence from a study by Oliver *et al.* (1985) highlights this. They report that out of 596 people with severe learning difficulties who also have self-injuring behaviours identified in the south-east Thames region, only 12 were receiving any form of psychological treatment and only 11 (2 per cent) were receiving any behavioural treatment.

The intervention

Over the past 15 years, there have been major advances in the teaching of new appropriate skills to people with these characteristics. This work has been led in the United States by Lovaas, Foxx, Azrin, Koegel, Egel, Rincover, Carr and others, and these methods are already being used in the UK by highly specialist professionals, for a tiny minority of the people concerned, in particular in the four specialist units already mentioned.

The intervention package developed in Southampton by the Health Care Evaluation Research Team has built on these advances and has modified and simplified them for use, under professional supervision, by parents at home, teachers at school and care assistants in short-term residential care units.

The intervention is designed not only to teach carers how to gain a basic degree of necessary compliance to teach the person with severe learning difficulties positive new skills, but also to teach all direct carers how to enable the people with severe learning difficulties to practise the age-appropriate skills they have, by participating at all times and in all settings in all of the activities which constitute the normal daily routine, in a way which improves the overall quality of life for the people with severe learning difficulties themselves, and for those who care for them in all settings. Relevant age-appropriate tasks are practised so that people with learning difficulties can eventually acquire skills relevant to their active participation from getting up until going to bed – with differing ranges of additional guidance and help from parents, teachers, residential care workers or external workers – in the widest possible range of 'normal' activities, i.e. in 'doing' the activity and also in the preparation and tidying of such activities. This is achieved through those people with primary responsibilities for caring directly for them, who are taught to follow procedures designed specifically to help the people with learning difficulties achieve agreed specific objectives of mastering their environment in age-appropriate ways.

Through the acquisition of new age-appropriate skills, an increase in age-appropriate engaged behaviour, and a decrease in inappropriate and challenging behaviours, people spending time in any environment may do so with more enjoyment and less stress for those caring for them.

Also a greater number of people with challenging behaviours may be enabled to live in ordinary, little-restricted environments at home or elsewhere, without having to be confined permanently to residential or day environments which have special facilities which are also restrictive, and congregate such people in the same setting. It is important to note that since such children are inevitably growing into adolescents and adults, success from early interventions could help these people as adults to live and participate for the rest of their lives in unrestricted living and work places, and in further education settings.

The intervention developed by the Health Care Evaluation Research Team can be seen as a natural progression from, or an addition to, the Portage home teaching package. With the Portage system, parents with no specialist educational training are now effectively teaching their pre-school children with severe learning difficulties new age-appropriate skills, and controlling some of their difficult behaviours, during formal teaching sessions, in the presence of a rapidly trained non-specialist home teacher (Smith *et al.*, 1977). However, such parents still have difficulty in carrying out teaching procedures in formal and informal sessions even with pre-school children who emit severely disruptive behaviours. In addition, despite Portage teaching, these children make very few positive skill gains and tend to maintain their disruptive behaviours (Smith *et al.*, *ibid.*). Thus, in spite of the widespread success of the Portage intervention in its implementation and results, this group of children with severe learning difficulties and severely challenging behaviours is not adequately provided for by the package.

In 1982 a research project was therefore set up under the auspices of the DHSS, to develop a home intervention with children and young adults with severe and profound learning difficulties and with severely challenging behaviours, such as self-injury, aggression, disruption and non-compliance. This uses behavioural procedures and materials based on the work of Lovaas *et al.* (1981) and Koegel *et al.* (1977 and 1978). Because of evidence that adults caring for such people experienced considerable stress which impeded their maintenance of procedures, the package includes cognitive behavioural modification procedures. The aim of the project was to produce, in manual form, procedures which had been developed and tested initially in relation to a small number of families and the relevant direct care personnel. This could then be made available, together with training video-tapes, to individuals, services and units who wished to use or field test the intervention package.

After working mainly with the parents, teachers and residential care staff in relation to four families, this project (which ended on 31st December 1985 at the termination of the DHSS grant period) achieved its major objectives. With each successive family (and the relevant carers at school and in the residential units) major goals were attained increasingly quickly and effectively in relation to people with challenging behaviour of increasing severity. The goals of the intervention are in essence threefold. First, that the parents, teachers and residential unit staff caring for people with severe and profound learning difficulties who live at home and who emit severely aggressive, self-injurious, self-stimulating, disruptive and/or non-compliant behaviours, will have practised, in role play, behaviour modification procedures which they can implement successfully direct with people for whom they care, not only during short periods of formal teaching but throughout the day in all normal activities such as eating, toileting, bathing, dressing and undressing, getting up and going to bed and during leisure time, as well as in the preparation and tidying-up of these activities. The extent to which this goal is attained largely determines the amount of time spent by the person with severe learning difficulties in engaged and age-appropriate behaviours, and thereby (a) improves the quality of life for the person and the carers involved, and (b) allows less time and opportunity for people to perform disruptively and in a self-stimulating manner and (c) constitutes repeated learning trials for the person to acquire effective direct-teaching and caring skills. Secondly, the teachers at the schools and education centres these people attend apply the essential procedures of behaviour modification throughout the day, using them to integrate the people with severe learning difficulties into the normal activities of the school or centre and of the other people in the class or group, i.e. the people concerned, despite their very severe learning difficulties and very challenging behaviours, take an active part, with help and guidance when necessary, in the 'normal' day. Thirdly, residential care workers in the short-term residential care units (in which these people spend a varying amount of the week while continuing to be based at home) also learn the same procedures, and, whenever possible, carry them out in all activities throughout the day, as at home. Thus, for the people with severe learning difficulties themselves, there are specific objectives relating to their daily life that can be summarized in the following way.

1 For short periods of the day they will follow special teaching programmes to learn new skills, which are age-appropriate, and will also follow programmes to unlearn the skills which are not age-appropriate – in particular to decrease their challenging behaviours which include self-injury, aggression, destructiveness or disruptiveness.

2 For the major part of the day they will actively take part in routine activities such as getting up, toileting, eating, dressing, bathing, formal education, i.e. in the preparation, doing, and the tidying up associated with these activities.

3 For very brief periods of the day they will be involved in various programmes such as physiotherapy, speech therapy and take appropriate medicines which are aimed at helping them to attain their desired objectives.

These objectives are widely believed to be highly relevant to the achievement of a high quality of life by all people, whether or not they have physical impairments, severe learning difficulties or severely challenging behaviours.[1]

The intervention steps

The length and detail of the programme will vary to some extent in each individual case but overall it follows a standard pattern. The stages, from first contact with the parents, until the end of the major intensive training week will take approximately three months.

1 The referral meeting

When a person is referred (most probably by their GP or paediatrician, teacher, instructor or residential care worker) a meeting is held by the

[1]A handbook detailing the methods and accompanied by illustrative video-tapes is in progress.

supervisor with the referring professional and the parents. At this meeting the programme is described and video film is shown of some basic steps. The parents are then given about a week to decide for themselves whether or not they want to get involved. Allowing them time to consider is designed to avoid their making hasty decisions in the first flush of enthusiasm at the meeting.

2 First interviews

If they do decide to continue, the parents are then interviewed at length to get detailed descriptions and discussion in three main areas:

(a) the current activities of the person with severe learning difficulties and other members of the family, from getting up in the morning to going to bed at night;
(b) how the parents would like the day to be, and how, ideally, the daily activities would proceed, if the targets in relation to the very challenging behaviours of their child were to be attained;
(c) the current strengths of their child, i.e. age-appropriate things he or she can do at the moment, and which it is important that he or she continues to do in the future; the current excesses, i.e. the behaviours which now occur too frequently and which the parents would like to reduce, e.g. self-mutilating, screaming, kicking, etc.; the current deficits, i.e. the things the person cannot do now, which are age-appropriate, and if developed, would be in his or her, and the carers', best interests.

At these initial interviews, developmental checklists are also filled in to record the person's current social, verbal, physical and self-help skills. Similar interview procedures are followed in relation to the school teachers, teaching assistants, social educators and the residential care workers involved; this also includes the current situation, and how they would prefer it to be at each point throughout the day, when they are in charge of the person.

3 Baseline videoing

Videoing then takes place at home, at school, in the social education centre and in the residential unit to record what is actually happening in these settings. The carers are asked what they consider to be their 'best times' with the person with challenging behaviours and their 'worst times', and these are subsequently filmed. The carers are also filmed giving a set of basic direction-following instructions such as 'Come here', 'Look at me' and 'Sit down', as well as any particular instructions that the caring adult had indicated on the developmental checklist that the person normally follows.

This video material is vitally important since it provides the baseline data of the interaction pattern between the caring adult and the person with severe learning difficulties. Its analysis and comparison with similar data collected during and after the programme is the main form of assessment of changes in the interaction between the person and the caring adult.

4 Professionals' meetings

At this stage, and every two to three months from then onwards, a meeting is held with all the professionals involved (as detailed earlier) and the parents. At this first meeting, video film of baseline conditions is shown and its analysis is discussed. The parents tell the meeting how they would like things to change. They outline their new objectives for their child and state briefly how they plan to attain their objectives. The professionals are given further information about the programme by the supervisor, and the teachers and residential care staff present are invited to support the agreed objectives for the person with severe learning difficulties, and to agree to work towards attaining them in their own settings.

5 Workshops and role play

Three-day workshops are held, first at home and then in other settings, without the person with challenging behaviour present. These begin with a general discussion about the relationship between the emotional state of caring adults and the importance of their being able to create their own calm (and to avoid excessive anger, depression and anxiety) in order to respond effectively to very challenging behaviours of some people with severe learning difficulties. The parents (and other direct carers) are encouraged to talk openly about how they feel, and to explore ways of exercising control over this by noting the relationship between their feelings and their beliefs. They are also encouraged to identify what their long-term objectives are both for themselves and for the person for whom they care. The discussions are followed by videotapes showing role play of the basic curriculum. Role play then begins, initially between one parent and the supervisor, and then between the parents themselves, with each one alternately role playing their 'child'.

The basic curriculum consists of a distillation of the core skills developed by Lovaas, Egel, Koegel and others, working in clinics under laboratory conditions, or in specialist units for training caring adults to teach people with severe learning difficulties and severely challenging behaviours.

At the beginning of the role play sessions parents, teachers and care assistants are taught to teach the 'person' the core curriculum of direction-following by using the following procedures:

(a) getting attention, eye contact and stilling, before giving an instruction;
(b) giving any instruction loudly, clearly, simply, consistently and once only, i.e. without repetition (without nagging);
(c) if the instruction is not carried out after five seconds while standing or sitting still (or earlier if the person moves away, or behaves disruptively) physically prompting the person effectively, i.e. until the task instructed is carried out;
(d) conspicuously celebrating successes and providing effective rewards, and conspicuously ignoring or clearly correcting failure to carry out the task;[1]
(e) keeping trials discrete, i.e. not asking for a second task until the first is completed.

From the caring adult's perspective the core curriculum of direction following consists of a simple sequence of instructions. They are:

Look at me! (unless blind, in which case some alternative method of gaining attention is used)
Sit down!
Hands quiet!
Do ....! (i.e. carry out a task while sitting)
Stand up!
Stand up straight!
Hands quiet!
Do ....! (i.e. carry out a task while standing)

From the perspective of the person being instructed, the core curriculum consists of following the instruction given, without help or with decreasing degrees of help.

The role play is first carried out with the adult role playing the person with challenging behaviours very well and then becoming more and more difficult, acting out all the possible kinds of behaviour that can be expected of the actual person concerned. When this is being dealt with effectively and confidently in one-to-one settings, the adults role play a situation in which another person is also present, demanding attention to different degrees. They then role play coping with two such additional people and complete the additional task of filling in record sheets relating to following instructions, the occurances of disruptive behaviours, etc. This ensures that all procedures are individually designed and role played (initially with the parents and later with the other professionals) before being applied directly with the person with severe learning difficulties. If more than mildly aversive procedures

---

[1]Non-aversive or minimally aversive procedures to be used in the event of severely self-injurious behaviours are dealt with in detail in the handbook.

are to be used or if these are any doubts about aversive or restrictive procedures the proposals are considered by an ethical committee of experienced professionals, parents and legal representatives.

6 Intensive training

Once the adults have reached criterion in teaching in role play, the intensive training begins, working directly with the person with challenging behaviours, in a series of three five-day workshops in the home, school or social education centre and residential unit. The parents (and then teachers and residential care workers) are taught to carry out the procedures ((a) – (e) above) in the basic core curriculum and then to apply them in relation to all the daily activities – toileting, dressing, bathing, getting up and going to bed, eating, playing and so on. The person with challenging behaviours is involved actively in the actual activities and also in the preparation and tidying-up of each activity, e.g. in relation to eating, laying the table, getting food out of the cupboard, wiping the table, washing up plates, etc. Apart from basic routine activities the caring adults are encouraged to suggest and implement new tasks to be taught and carried out. Particular problem areas such as messy eating, refusal to sit at table, urinating on the floor and so on, are tackled 'en passant' during this intensive training week, by using the basic procedures of getting attention, giving instructions and prompts, corrections, etc. In addition particular strategies are prepared and tried out for dealing with specifically difficult behaviours like self-injury or assaultive behaviour. At school, teachers and teaching assistants, after attaining the basic objectives in relation to eating and toileting, begin to integrate the child into the activities of the class as a whole by applying the core procedures to all activities. Residential care workers in their own setting also tackle eating and toileting and dressing before going on to any other routine activities they wish to include in the person's daily activity schedule. Particular attention is paid to non-punitive procedures in overcoming or managing the person's challenging behaviours.

Activity schedules and record keeping

A key component of non-punitive procedures, since people with severe learning difficulties, at the outset, are unable to arrange their own activities, is the structuring of meaningful activities throughout the working day.[1]

[1]As soon as they are able to participate in the selection of preferred materials, people with severe learning difficulties should begin participating in the planning of their own activity schedules. Whenever possible people who are unable to plan their own activity are offered a choice of two activities.

This is achieved by the introduction of activity schedules* which are drawn up daily or weekly.[1] They indicate which activity is to occur, and with which allocated carer, every half an hour. This positive programmimg sets the occasion for structured activity which gives many opportunities for positive reinforcement of behaviours.

Whenever possible, carers working with people with very challenging behaviours should only work for half-hourly periods and then be relieved by someone else.* Written schedules are intended to ensure that this happens, and that the person is engaged in some sort of planned, meaningful activity throughout most of the day. Carefully planned record keeping enables systematic monitoring in the context of specific teaching programmes, and in relation to frequency and duration of episodes of challenging behaviours. An agreed arrangement is required that, if a carer in charge of a group of people with challenging behaviours has to work one-to-one with such a person behaving disruptively, the other people in the group will automatically be taken over by another caring adult.* This is likely to remove much of the stress felt by the caring adults who are accountable for groups of people which include some with very challenging behaviours.

The Southampton study

The full sequence of interventions, as outlined above, evolved out of work with five families. Most of the sequence was carried out in Southampton in relation to two children, four parents, fifteen teachers and assistants and eight residential workers. The first three cases have been described elsewhere (Kushlick *et al.*, 1985).

The case of J

J was 12 years old when first referred to the HCERT team by the consultant psychiatrist in mental handicap. Born without any signs of neuropathology or signs of learning disability, J suffered severe encephalopathy following a whooping cough immunization at six months. From then on he showed profound learning disability and his challenging behaviours presented an increasing problem to his parents. He developed few skills, very slowly, and his screaming was described as 'incessant'. At three years old he was reported to rock, scream and self-mutilate – he banged his head on objects and broke window panes with his head.

Over the years various drugs and behavioural interventions had been tried with him. Sometimes these were reported to have been effective in specific areas. For example, in 1976 a programme using aversion therapy (a squirt of

---

[1]Procedures marked with an asterisk have not been used, but could be followed in any future intervention.

water in the face) was used at mealtime at the residential unit because J repeatedly threw his spoon and food, and sometimes the whole bowl. The warden of the unit reported (November 1977) that 'after four months and much improvement during mealtime behaviour, the programme was extended to ordinary daytime activities, with continued improvement.' There is no further report mentioning this aversion therapy, and a later report from the residential unit (December 1982) states that 'on a good day J is capable of eating nicely, without bolting his food. On a bad day ... J will wave his spoon about, eat rapidly, spilling food everywhere, grab at other peoples' food', etc. In 1977 a 'rapid toilet training procedure' based on methods used by Foxx and Azrin (1977) was carried out in the residential unit. It was reported (warden's report, *ibid.*) that as a result, J only wore nappies at night. However, in 1984, he was wearing nappies all day and night at the residential unit. Reports of improvements after changes of drugs are vague and unsubstantiated 'J had a change of drugs in January and he generally appeared a happier child in himself and was more responsive' (school report, 1982). 'A course of Epilim did help his behaviour in the past but a recent trial has not helped' (GP, 1982). An additive free diet was suggested in December 1982 and in April 1983 the consultant paediatrician wrote: 'I am pleased to say that the diet ... seems to have had a dramatic effect. His parents came in and announced that the boy's psoriasis is cured, that his behaviour is better and that his concentration span has improved enormously. He is having far fewer of his fit-like outbursts.' Again, two months later, he wrote: 'I was delighted to see (6.6.83) that, on his additive free diet, he remains free of his awful self-destructive behaviour and his face has completely healed up. The psoriasis remains completely quiescent.' In 1984, however, when the present intervention began, J was still on the diet, but was head hitting, and suffering from psoriasis.

At no time have there been reports of changes in the topographies of J's positive behaviours, and there are no reports of suggestions that his behavioural excesses were controllable if specific procedures were followed.

In June, 1984, at 12 years old, J was still living at home, in spite of frequent advice from a number of professionals to 'put him away'. His behaviours included combinations and permutations of banging his head with his fist (causing damage to the soft tissues and drawing blood), shouting, falling, grabbing and resisting. Although the tendency to self-injury appeared to vary at different times of the year, at those times at which these behaviours did occur they often followed demands that J did things he preferred not to do. Less frequently they occurred when his attempts to gain attention were being ignored and occasionally as a self-stimulatory behaviour. Despite past interventions J still did very little for himself and no systematic demands were made on him to prepare or tidy up after activities. Most of the time at home he was being entertained with songs, nursery rhymes or toys, or being processed or restrained. He attended a special school where he had been described as 'unteachable', and at the time the intervention began, spent most of the time in school wandering around the class room, which contained older and much more able children grabbing and misusing their materials. Much of the interaction between J and the staff consisted of restraining J from self-injury or from removing the materials of the other children. He was excluded from many routine activities such as eating in the dining hall, cooking, gardening, register taking, attending the tuckshop and other activities at school and outside. From Friday afternoon until Monday morning he stayed in a residential care unit where he also spent school holidays.

At this stage he had very few self-help skills other than sitting, at home, in a restraining chair and feeding himself with a spoon, very quickly and messily. He woke very early in the morning, often at 3 or 4 am. His mother woke up when he did and stayed with him from that time onwards, for fear of what he might do if left on his own. She amused him from the time he woke until he went to school at 9 o'clock, singing nursery rhymes and playing babyish games with him, except during eating, washing and toileting and dressing activities. Toileting, which was usually a long and stressful period, took place in a special toileting chair in his room. Dressing involved following him around from room to room. In his bath he splashed vigorously, slipping out of control and drinking the bath water. When he came home at 3.15 pm in the afternoon his mother again spent long hours amusing him until he went to sleep, which could be any time up to midnight, though sometimes he was asleep by nine. Often he had to be carried upstairs to his bedroom where it would take from half an hour to five hours to fall asleep, pacing his bedroom until he fell asleep. His mother chose to sit with him for as long as it took him to go to sleep. Occasionally he did not sleep at all, and when this happened his mother stayed up with him all night. He was doubly incontinent, although his mother was able to interpret the signs (a puffing, heavy breathing) when he wanted to go to the toilet, so that in general there were ways of limiting accidents at home.

He had no speech and very little apparent receptive language. He was receiving a low dose of Serenace (Haloperidol), and was on an additive free diet, which was said to have made a dramatic reduction in his head hitting and psoriasis for at least five months, when first introduced early in 1983. It was also believed to improve the allergic conjunctivitis which afflicted him during the spring and summer months. Not surprisingly it failed to set the occasion for new positive behaviours or for reducing the excesses of falling on the floor, giggling, self-stimulation or wandering around grabbing things.

The intervention with J's family and carers began in June 1984. Video material of sample sequences of routine activities at different times of the day and in all settings was collected at baseline and throughout the intervention, and follow-up film was taken over a period of a year after the intensive 15-day (five days in each setting) direct teaching programme (which took place in October 1984). These were used to provide feedback to the parents and other direct care staff on how they were implementing the agreed direct teaching procedures and also to illustrate errors and ways of performing appropriate procedures. They were also used to develop and test systematic ways of measuring meaningful changes and to assist the carers to teach the people with severe learning difficulties. Systematic quantitative analysis using these measures is currently in progress. This chapter presents results relating to easily observable differences in the topographies of the behaviour of the caring adults, of J himself, before and after the intervention package was applied. The description aims to illustrate the *quality* of change which took place in different activities and in different settings at *some* times of the day and some periods of the intervention. They are not quantitative data on the degree to which these changes were maintained at all times of the day over the whole period, and in all settings. There is no doubt that, at home, there have been important changes for J and his mother in the activities both of them do during the day and in the way in which they interact.

During the intensive training period J's parents were encouraged actively to use the basic direct teaching procedures to involve J in the preparation, doing and tidying of all activities in his daily routine. As a direct result, immediately after the intervention, and for nearly 18 months since, instead of spending long hours between his toileting, dressing and eating activities (with no preparation or tidying up) amusing him continuously with nursery rhymes and age-inappropriate toys, to distract him and to avoid 'provoking' disruptive and self-injurious behaviour, his mother involved him in preparatory and cleaning up procedures connected with all routine household activities, giving clear and effective reinforcement of age-appropriate behaviour. Thus breakfast time now consisted of J (on discrete trial instruction, with prompts where necessary and with clear social and other reinforcements) opening cupboards, taking out the cereal, closing the cupboard, fetching the milk and sugar, pouring the food out, and so on, and then, after eating, helping with the washing, drying and putting away of his bowl. At school, too, immediately after the intervention and for some months following, J was taking part in the daily routines of the classroom, doing (with help) a range of activities with the rest of the children in the class, including such things as responding to the register, taking part in formal teaching sessions, queueing for tuck, gardening, mixing food for cooking, painting and doing music and movement. In many of these he was involved in preparation and tidying of materials. He had previously been excluded from these activities because of the self-injurious and disruptive behaviours (head hitting, shouting, falling on the floor, running away) which he emitted when instructed, prompted and corrected. Whereas he had previously eaten his meals in the classroom (eating sandwiches with his fingers), he now joined 60 children in the dining room and ate a cooked meal with a spoon using the procedures introduced at home. In the residential unit, where the direct carers and other staff perceived the monitoring activities as very aversive, the basic procedures were used consistently for two months after the training and less consistently thereafter during dressing, toileting, bathing and eating, though leisure activities were never programmed. In early January 1985 residential care staff requested that video monitoring at getting up time in the morning and at meal times stop, and a month later vetoed all videoing in the unit. Eight months later (in September 1985) video monitoring of leisure and bathing was allowed again. Direct monitoring was allowed throughout until the end of the grant period. The staff report that he now sits for longer periods (with other children who are watching television) and that his eating has improved, since the intervention.

One of J's most difficult and distressing behaviours, head hitting, occurs cyclically, i.e. even without special interventions it decreases or stops 'spontaneously'. During the intensive training period he was not head hitting at all, but began again shortly afterwards, and methods for dealing with it which were practised during role play, i.e. shouting 'No! Hands quiet', and roughly correcting him physically, were tried unsuccessfully. In December 1984 'required relaxation', as described and recommended (but not tested) by Foxx and Azrin (1972) and by Webster and Azrin (1973) in the USA to be applied with people who failed to sit still and relax on their own, was tried. When J was hitting his head at a rate of two per second or more he was made to lie on his back on the floor, his head resting on a pillow, and with his hands held on the floor above his head. He was held there with as much force as required to hold him still until he relaxed for ten seconds while still being gently held with minimal force. The hands were then removed completely and he then had to lie on the floor, relaxed and without moving, for a further ten seconds. He was then praised and instructed to get up and return to the task he had been engaged in before the required relaxation procedure. At first, this procedure took about between 20 and 30 minutes, but soon decreased to about four or five minutes at home and at school. Residential care staff resisted using it until July 1985 when the person in charge took the training and also suggested a new method of holding J when he resisted for long periods. By midsummer, however, the technique was becoming too difficult to implement (as described) because of J's prolonged resistance to it, and our fears that he might be injured. Although still used at times, his parents (and the staff at school and in the residential unit) were finding that J struggled so hard that they were unable to hold him down. Detailed observation also showed that it was being used inconsistently and inaccurately, i.e. being started too late and terminated too early. For a short time a new method was brought in, with J lying on his front with his arms held either on the floor or behind his back. This was used sporadically over the next few months. The records showed that J was taking increasingly longer to relax in this position (up to 40 – 50 minutes) and because of the escalation of J's physical resistance (and thus of possible injury) and because of concern for establishing more positive topographies which could be differentially reinforced, it was stopped. J's parents returned to the use of an earlier version of required relaxation, sitting J on the sofa with one parent on either side of him, or one parent holding down his arms from a standing position in front of him. At school he was put on a chair and two members of staff sat either side of him holding one arm each. If staff were not available to do this J was, as before, restrained in a chair with straps to hold him.

From June of 1985, it became clear that the research was not to be funded in the future, and there was no clear service department available to take over the supervision of the intervention when the research team withdrew formal supervisory procedures. In the absence of any special supervision and monitoring procedures the situation, nine months later, is that J's parents continue to use the procedures systematically with him at all times of the day. In other settings systematic use of the procedures has now largely ceased, though plans are in hand for reinstating them within the ordinary service structure. At school, J tends to spend much of the day sitting in his chair watching the others in the class, rather than taking part in the activities himself. One-to-one work with him occurs infrequently. He still eats a full meal in the dining-hall using a normal spoon (as at home) and he continues to participate in some activities when he is not in his chair, and when staff familiar with direct teaching procedures, use them. He is described by his teachers and by professionals who have visited the school over many years, as calmer and more under control than he was before the intervention began nearly a year and a half ago.

When he is in the residential unit (and not involved in dressing, toileting, bathing or eating) J continues to spend a great part of the day walking from one room to another, weaving his arms in stereotypic fashion, thumb-biting or giggling. He makes eye contact with and smiles at children or adults and sits watching television for short periods. There have never been systematically scheduled activities for him other than getting up, dressing, toileting, bathing, eating, and going to bed and J has never been involved in preparation and tidying up in this setting, and this situation continues. The adult interaction rate with him remains very low. When he hits his head the staff follow a strategy of ignoring him, and on occasion he is put in a room on his own until head hitting and shouting stop. Some of the components of required relaxation are applied irregularly on occasion.

In all settings (and particularly at home), when the appropriate procedures are followed in relation to a schedule of relevant activities, J follows these with varying degrees of help and enthusiasm, and at most times the carers appear calm and confident in their management procedures. Parents, teaching staff and an educational psychologist are involved in planning further activities at school. Members of the hospital management team have expressed commitment to continuing the procedures, to developing them in their settings and to supporting them in other settings. So far no supervisory routines have been set up.

The analysis of the intervention with J has highlighted certain unresolved problems. Even among parents (such at J's) who have shown the greatest commitment to the intervention, detailed analysis of the teaching interaction at the height of the training shows that it fails to attain the criteria set by Koegel *et al.* (1977). There are only a small proportion of interactions in which J's attention (eye contact, stilling and quiet hands) is obtained before an instruction is given, and only a small proportion of instructions are given to J without him being held because of his tendency to walk away, drop to the ground, shuffle his feet or flap his arms. Although the instructions given by the mother are often clear, loud, single and not repeated, it can be seen that these can seldom be followed by a prompt (after five seconds) because J behaves in such a way that a correction has to be given instead. Because of the strength and high frequency of these escape and self-stimulating behaviours, it is extremely difficult to reinforce J's appropriate behaviours without also simultaneously reinforcing inappropriate, self-stimulatory or escape behaviours. If a reinforcer is given it is often likely, unless given immediately, to follow a subsequent inappropriate response.

The case of C

C was first referred to the team in January 1984, a month before her eighth birthday. She has severe learning disabilities and a wide range of severely disruptive and aggressive behaviours. She seldom stood or sat still for more than a few minutes, even to eat her meals, which she sometimes ate on the floor. She hit out at other people, sometimes very hard, especially at strangers and other children. She also quickly produced large amounts of mucus from her nose directly on to people or objects or she smeared it on people and furniture. She made loud, unintelligible noises, clapped her hands much of the time, and usually failed to follow directions given to her to do things like 'Come here', 'Give me ...', 'Put this ...'. When her whining became very aversive the parents would send her to her bedroom where she would rock, clap her hands, whine and kick the wall for long periods.

The programme carried out with C was, in the beginning, restricted to getting her to follow the core curriculum of simple direction-following while sitting down, i.e. in formal educational situations. Parents, teachers and residential care workers carried out the procedures (in order to gain educational control) in one setting in short sessions each day. Later the procedures were generalized to other settings within the house. Still later, in March 1985, new intensive training sessions of the form used with J were held at home and at C's school and residential unit in order to extend the use of the core direct teaching procedures to all activities at all times of the day.

The programme with C began, as with J, with the basic curriculum of simple direction following. When she was following this competently, her parents, teachers and residential care staff widened her curriculum to include, sequentially, gross motor imitation, fine motor imitation, simple sounds and then words. Unlike J, C showed rapid signs of learning the new skills which were now being taught to her. By June 1985 she was able to name objects, and went on to name objects in pictures and subsequently to identify colours. At home, she was encouraged to name objects she used in routine activities, such as 'flannel' and 'toothbrush'. At school, she is now included in group teaching, and will identify pictures while a member of a group. Her parents report that she now spontaneously verbalizes, and is able to carry out increasingly complex instructions and can dress and undress herself, lay the table, eat with utensils at the table and so on.

This progress in verbal and self-help skills has occurred despite the continued presence of her aggressive and noisy behaviours, including hitting, kicking and smearing mucus. These occur mainly with adults who do not follow the procedures and with other children. Her parents are very pleased with her progress in terms of education and self-help skills, but believe, and express disappointment, that her negative behaviours, including the bedroom behaviours, have hardly improved at all. They have now decided, for a number of reasons, that C should go into permanent care.

The teaching procedures were implemented, and the progress occurred, despite the fact that regular scheduled activities have not been used throughout the day, and that intensive schedules of positive reinforcement of non-problem behaviours have not been followed systematically. No correction or required relaxation procedures have been followed systematically, and her parents (and school and residential care staff) have insisted that no aversive procedures other than 'time out' standing in a corner of the room, or hand holding for a minute following an aggressive act, are to be used.

Maintenance and development

After early gains in effective educational control, the targets of maintenance and creative development of the procedures, as the child reacts with increasing degrees of resistance, are the most challenging and difficult to attain. Two years after the first meetings held to set up the intervention, all those involved at all levels and in all settings still express verbal support for the objectives of the intervention, but, in practice, at school and in the residential unit many of the procedures (which have been seen to achieve agreed objectives) have been dropped. However, despite the lack of any continued special monitoring by the research team, and despite the delay in setting up an alternative monitoring system, the staff in J's residential unit and school have not reverted completely to the patterns of behaviour that existed before the intervention began. However, even a few weeks after the intensive training programme, which concentrated entirely on one-to-one procedures, the residential unit staff reported to the research team that they felt stressed carrying out the procedures with J regularly, mainly because they believed that there were too few staff and that the other children would suffer if they gave too much time to J. Although they reported that J was generally calmer, and ate less messily since the intervention, they simultaneously expressed dissatisfaction at not being able to do the procedures as well as they wanted to, and criticized the procedures as being more intensive than they felt they could manage. No one doubted that J would profit from more frequent teaching trials. They were reluctant, in the present climate of cuts, to ask management for any further staff. From the point of view of the child and the parents it is important that some professional carers, for whatever reason, spoke negatively about, and stopped carrying out, key components of the programme. Further work will be required to find ways of arranging managerial and professional leadership, and local working conditions of caring staff, which support and motivate direct carers to implement required procedures over long periods, and which attempt to overcome the very real challenges presented.

The value for the child of consistent, effective teaching trials in relation to all routine activities is demonstrated by the new positive behavioural topographies which were elicited with guidance, in both children, and the new skills (especially of expressive language) learned by one of them. The programme with J demonstrates that children (and adults) with severe or profound learning difficulties and challenging behaviours may be able, given help and guidance, to follow instructions systematically and therefore begin to participate routinely in a very wide range of activities and settings. The results with C show that they may also gain new positive skills and require less instruction, prompting and reinforcing when using them. In order to maintain self-help and educational skills, and to teach new ones, it is likely that very carefully scheduled activities are needed. Activity schedules relating to each half hour of the day could assist carefully monitored staff to arrange materials and activities, so that the people in their care achieve high levels of active engagement during their waking day (Felce and de Kock, 1983). In addition parents and staff need sustained guidance, resources and support, at all levels, to accept completely, at any time, their own behaviours and those of the people for whom they care, to accept responsibility for helping to create the conditions and the behaviours they prefer in relation to those for whom they care, and to maintain enthusiasm and positive attitudes in the face of work which is frequently characterized as very tiring and monotonous. The allocation of resources to sustain a varied and interesting schedule of instructional activities for people with high frequency challenging behaviours must be a priority if the use of very expensive, undesirable (and ineffective) measures such as very aversive contingencies, and doses of tranquillizers at life-threatening levels are to be avoided. In addition monitoring and careful management is required to ensure that caring staff undertake this demanding one-to-one work with people with challenging behaviours for limited periods only (e.g. half-hour sessions) and are automatically relieved of group work when difficult behaviour arises which needs to be dealt with using one-to-one procedures.

In the current project it has only been possible to observe and begin to attempt (just before the project ended) to deal with some of the problems of development and maintenance which have arisen. It is obvious from this project (and from many other studies in various countries) that the long-term development and maintenance of effective, imaginative and non-punitive procedures – however 'difficult' or 'boring' they are characterized as – in order to enable people with such challenging behaviours to experience and master a wide range of environments available to all people, must be seen as the main objective of any service for people with very challenging behaviours.

One target which has not been achieved at this stage of the intervention is the precise following of the direct teaching components during structured teaching. At this stage no method has been found of getting J to sit still long enough to take hands off him during instruction. Also, it is still difficult to reinforce his appropriate behaviours without also reinforcing his intrusive inappropriate behaviours. The methods of making progress in these areas will involve the very detailed analysis of teaching sequences (which will overcome these errors) which are then practised in the context of simulations of the daily routine. The effectiveness of these role-play sequences in achieving the required objectives will be reflected in the results of the coded analyses.

Another area in which the intervention is still unsuccessful is in the complete elimination of self-stimulation and aggressive or self-injurious behaviour during direct teaching sessions. Methods used with J to control head hitting during direct-teaching sessions were completely successful for a limited period, but his resistance to required relaxation procedures increased until continued restraint could have resulted in injury. A promising recent development in methods of overcoming difficult behaviours, which has not been tested at this stage of the intervention, has been suggested by Lovett (1985). This approach uses 'paradoxical intention' contingencies, i.e. when escape or other disruptive behaviour functions occur spontaneously, they are consciously requested (i.e. brought under instructional control) so that they can then be positively reinforced, over a number of trials, until satiation occurs. The reinforcer of anger in a caring adult is lost and the behaviour functions as a mild punisher. These procedures would be useful if they helped to avoid escalation of confrontations, and would increase the range of opportunities to give positive reinforcement. Also, at this stage, no fall-back procedures have been tested for the use of splints and other mechanical restraints, or powerful tranquillizers as life-saving procedures when all other methods proved ineffective.

Conclusions

It is clear that in order even to begin to maintain skills and positive behaviour patterns over time, adequate resources must be made available to support direct caring adults and enable effective procedures to be continued. A key objective, however difficult, is to help providers to value the people with challenging behaviours, and their active participation in all routine activities, in all settings, and also to provide and maintain resources for them. These people are often considered to be of low worth and the implementation of effective procedures is too readily characterized by people (without direct experience of them *or* their outcomes) as having low worth, e.g. boring, repetitive, unimaginative, authoritarian or even inhuman.

It is important to help professionals and managers to understand that human services are effective to the extent that they widen their clients' experience and mastery of the universe in which they live. It would be good, though it is by no means essential, if the services, quite apart from the targets in relation to the people with challenging behaviours, were also to be a source of pleasure and creativity for the professionals and managers involved. This preliminary study has given further evidence that creative developments (making use of already existing procedures) can be used to achieve maintenance over time and across different settings, thus allowing people with severe learning difficulties to participate in a very wide range of activities, together with people of all repertoires, some of whom are specially allocated and trained to help avoid or overcome their disruptive behaviours, and to learn new skills. The curriculum of cognitive behaviour modification, made available as part of a general education for carers, may help them to keep up their morale and avoid unnecessary stress while they create new opportunities for themselves and for the people for whom they care. Guided by the ethical values of 'normalization', supported by recent gains in the recognition of the rights of people with challenging behaviours, and supported by political groupings committed to these objectives, it is now possible to refine the procedures for avoiding the self-defeating (and self-destructive) behaviours of some individuals, and for setting up and maintaining exciting alternatives.

Editors' note: Albert Kushlick and his team pioneered the research in England on the introduction of the Portage approach. In their chapter they discuss a development for severely disturbed and handicapped children. Society, through television and newspapers, has become acutely aware of the frequency of abuse of children in institutions and although the media constantly search for a scapegoat, it is felt by many psychologists that the very nature of institutionalization can create a situation which contributes to man's or woman's inhumanity to a fellow being. The chapter as well as covering a topical subject also addresses a very important problem and the Health Care Evaluation Research Team has once again researched and proposed a practical strategy for improving the current situation.

At the 1985 Portage Conference Albert Kushlick and his colleagues presented a videotape of the techniques described in this chapter and they very ably illustrated the behavioural approaches and the positive reactions from parents to the progress in their children. Many people who are not involved in the education of severely mentally handicapped children believe that just sending a pupil to a specialized institution is a guarantee that the pupil's needs will be adequately met. Sadly this is not the case and the Health Care Evaluation Research Team's work is therefore a major contribution which has considerable implications for the small group of people who are potential or actual victims of self-injurious or severely disabling behaviour. If the work is applied to the target population we may well see a considerable improvement in the morale of the specialized institutions as they experience the success now taken for granted by other exponents of the Portage model.

The chapter offers an exciting new challenge and since Dr Kushlick and his team have played such an important role in developing Portage in Great Britain and Northern Ireland as well as elsewhere, it is appropriate that the Health Care Evaluation Research Team's final project is reported in this book.

They Can't Mean Us: Criticism and Comments about Portage

R.J. Cameron

Introduction

The topic of 'education' is one on which few people would *not* hazard an opinion! As a result, everyone who works in the education sector has to put up with a ceaseless barage of views on how the present educational systems could be maintained, improved, redesigned or even scrapped.

Yet change in the educational world is slow and rarely seems to relate to the educational papers of various hues, educational debates of a greater or lesser nature and recommendations of both the tentative and forceful variety. Indeed most parents who renew their contact with the educational system, at a parents' evening in their child's secondary school for instance, are struck by the parallels and similarities between their own and their child's school life. To a casual observer it might sometimes appear that people in education had developed highly sophisticated strategies for avoiding the changes being thrust upon them, usually by waiting for today's recommendations to be replaced by the next equally sincerely advocated panacea. In education, the route from idea to action is strewn with the remains of many fascinating suggestions!

The big problem is that in all social systems, change, especially if it is for the better, is rarely attained without considerable inconvenience. The result has been that in the educational world, changes occur painfully slowly and tend to lag far behind the current state of knowledge in educational research.

A growth area

Yet, there is one section of education where a mini revolution has occurred over the past decade – the education of pre-school children with moderate and severe learning difficulties. Given the relatively slow pace of change in education, the speed of development of one particular approach – the Portage home teaching model – has been quite unusual. A potted history of Portage would read something as follows:

1969 US. Portage chosen as one of the 21 (out of 203) research proposals funded by the Bureau for the Education of the Handicapped under the Handicapped Children's Early Education Act.

1972 US. Office of Special Education provided funds for replication and effectiveness of the Portage model.
1975 US. Joint Dissemination and Review Panel of the United States Office of Education unanimously validated the Portage project as a model for dissemination and replication throughout the country.
1976 UK. Wessex and Welsh Portage research projects set up.
1980 UK. First National Portage Conference organized.
1983 UK. National Portage Association formed.
1984 US. Portage materials translated into eight different languages.
UK. More than 100 Portage services located in National Portage survey.
1985 UK. Department of Education and Science made £1.2 million from the education support grant available for setting up new Portage schemes in England and Wales.

There are two points to highlight in this short but dramatic historical overview. In the first place, some of the *educationally untypical* features of Portage – clear procedures, well-designed materials and a monitoring/evaluation component – do not appear to have aided replication in different cultural contexts. Secondly, the rapid development indicates that the Portage approach both identified and filled a *service vacuum* for families who had a pre-school child with special educational needs. (See Cameron, 1984.)

Evaluation

The relatively slow pace of change in education has already been mentioned. One other notable feature of our educational system is the lamentable lack of data on the effectiveness of services for pre-school handicapped children. Either the evidence for many services is sparse (as in the case in child guidance, paediatric, paramedical, psychological, etc., services) or it is inconclusive (as in the case of special schools, nursery education, residential care, etc.).

In sharp contrast, research evaluations of Portage services indicate encouraging outcomes for children and overwhelmingly positive consumer responses from parents. A selection of this evidence is set out in the Appendix and if we add the several dozen unpublished pilot and research studies carried out at a local level, it is difficult to disagree with the comment made by Lister (1985): 'there are few other examples of a system which has been so thoroughly evaluated and which has been so enthusiastically received by parents'.

Some criticisms

Successful ventures eventually attract critical comments. In the case of Portage, this has tended to be general criticism of the kind which can be applied to most pre-school intervention programmes. Many of these general comments have been challenged by Cameron *et al.* (1984) who conclude that Portage 'stands up remarkably well as a service delivery model for parents who have a preschool child with special needs'.

This conclusion does not however enshrine Portage as a model of perfection. On the contrary, constructive criticism of any service can encourage healthy new growth and development and is to be welcomed. However, it would be fair to say that some of the comments directed towards Portage have been of the less than constructive type and there is always a danger that some of these could obscure some of the glaring assets of the Portage model. In other words, we have to recognize that destructive comments can destroy the blossoms as well as the caterpillars!

It is therefore important to put criticism in context and to state that as far as Portage is concerned, major criticisms have been (a) remarkably sparse, (b) rarely backed up by hard evidence and (c) often pre-empted by new developments and additions to the Portage methodology. Although service delivery models like Portage may continue to attract some professional anxiety it is clear that this model has highlighted previously ignored opportunities for providing a constructive problem centred approach to families who have a child with special educational needs as well as opportunities for sharing and developing expertise among supporting professionals in the local authority and voluntary services.

Service complaints

Moving away from any critical comments which might have been made of the *general* Portage model, we might inquire about what (if any) opposition *individual* Portage services have faced at inception. Bendall (1985) posed this question in her National Portage survey and was able to conclude that it was 'more common for people to initiate a Portage type service against a background of disinterest and a lack of support (than against any opposition...)'.

Does this apparent professional apathy extend to the day-to-day operations of a Portage home teaching service? In Table 1, service complaints data obtained from the Winchester Portage home teaching service over a $9\frac{1}{2}$-year period is presented. During this period, 151 families received a Portage service and the agency problems listed here were raised at Portage staff meetings by home teachers. Such problems (and agreed action) were listed and monitored in the staff meeting minutes from which this data has been extracted.

In the case of the Winchester service, it can be seen that the majority of problems faced by the Portage team revolve around inter-professional cooperation, while most complaints about other supporting services are concerned with poor service delivery and problems involving school entry. It can also be noted in passing that more than three-quarters of the total agency problems discussed at staff meetings concern complaints made about supporting services *other than Portage*. (See Cameron, 1979, for further discussion.)

Table 1: A description of complaints about services for pre-school children with special educational needs raised at Portage staff meetings (April 1976 to September 1985)

Problem		Complaints about Portage		Complaints about other services
Lack of inter-professional cooperation		7		12
Inappropriate activities for children		6		5
Lack of information on children		5		0
School admission		0		20
Poor service delivery		3		37
Miscellaneous		3		0
	Total	24	Total	74

The distribution of 'complaint makers' shown in Table 2 illustrates the other interesting point that while complaints about the Portage service are made by a variety of supporting professionals (and a tiny minority of parents) *problems raised about other services came almost exclusively from parents* and tend to highlight some of the continuing problems in traditional services for families who have a handicapped pre-schooler. It is important also to note that as a Portage service becomes established and as communication networks with other support professionals and services are improved, then the number of problems which involve other agencies is likely to drop to a very low level (see Figure 1 for details).

Developing Portage

The original Portage model has proved itself to be remarkably robust. Components like criterion referenced assessment using the Portage checklist (Bluma *et al.*, 1976) the use of activity charts, continuous monitoring and record keeping survive almost unchanged from the original project which was developed in the early 1970s in Portage, Wisconsin (Shearer and Shearer, 1972). These and other aspects of Portage like curriculum planning and the management of disruptive behaviour have been considerably fattened up by ongoing action research.

Table 2: Complaints about services for pre-school children with special educational needs. Who makes these complaints?

(a)	*Complaints about Portage*	
	Paediatrician	6
	Headteacher	5
	Physiotherapist	2
	Speech therapist	2
	Home teacher	2
	Health visitor	2
	Parent	2
	Clinical medical officer	1
	Social worker	1
	Clinical psychologist	1
		Total 24
(b)	*Complaints about other services*	
	Home teachers	5
	Parents	69
		Total 74

Figure 1: Yearly frequency of complaints made about the Portage service in Winchester (1976 – 1985)

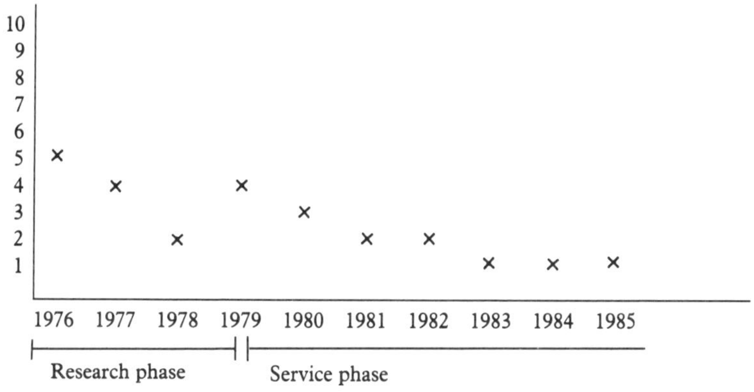

There has however been one other unusual aspect of the Portage service. The self-evaluation component has ensured that Portage became a dynamic (as opposed to static) model which attempted not only to maintain but to improve service delivery. As a result people working within Portage have not only been able to maintain and add to the original service delivery model, but have expanded the technology into new problem areas. In the remainder of this chapter, four exciting new areas of further development will be discussed. These are:

(a) Portage and non-educational problems
(b) Portage and profoundly handicapped children
(c) Portage and the teaching of early communication skills
(d) Portage and the quality of learning

Non-educational problems

> Portage needs to help parents with *their* difficulties as well as the children's (Russell, 1985)

> Perhaps we will never cease to care that our child is retarded (Philps, 1984)

In recommending the Portage service to other families with a handicapped child, parents have been at pains to stress the value of the practical help which they have received. However, they have additionally highlighted the fact that home teachers have helped them to tackle non-eductional problems especially family problems (see Smith *et al.*, 1977, Revill and Blunden, 1979 for details). It is clear therefore that parents can benefit from the home teaching component and the help with family problems which a regularly visiting home teacher can provide (Holland and Noaks, 1982, J. Cameron, 1984).

The need to extend the Portage methodology to include non-educational problems which occur within the family as a whole has been increasingly recognized by existing Portage services and has been vigorously championed by an enthusiastic group within the National Portage Association (see especially Dessent, 1984, Buckley, 1984, Le Poidevin and Cameron, 1985).

Suggestions on how the existing Portage model can be developed to help parents to deal with family problems have come from what are usually seen as two differing support systems – *Bereavement Counselling* and *Behavioural Psychology*. These two methodologies have been summarized in Figure 2 and despite the fact that they stem from quite different approaches to helping clients to deal with problems, the similarities are quite striking.

Figure 2: A comparison of two models for helping families to tackle non-educational/family problems: (a) the Bereavement Counselling Approach and (b) the Problem Centred Approach

The Bereavement Counselling Approach (After Le Poidevin, 1986)	*The Problem Centred Approach* (After Cameron, 1985)
Step 1 Opening	1 Assets and problem clarification
2 Getting the story	2 Selecting priorities
3 Summarizing themes	3 Examining controlling conditions
4 Setting goals	4 Setting objectives
5 Making the counselling contract	5 Agreeing strategy for change
6 Working through adjustment	6 Monitoring strategy for change
7 Evaluating outcome	7 Evaluating outcome
8 Closing	8 Renegotiating service delivery

Indeed, the possibility of combining the two approaches holds a number of attractions. In particular, the behaviourally orientated problem centred approach might gain from some of the subtle techniques in problem identification and clarification suggested by Le Poidevin (1986) while the counselling model could be considerably enhanced by drawing upon some of the well-established techniques in applied behaviour analysis developed to clarify the context in which problems occur and the strategies to enable clients to change their currrent responses to problem situations (see Cameron, 1985, for details).

When this interchange has been successfully completed, and when home teachers have been taught to use this approach successfully with parents, the Portage model will have received its most valuable addition to date. There is still a long way to go before Portage home teachers and parents can systematically tackle complex family problems but the early signs are promising!

Profoundly handicapped children

The difficulties of teaching profoundly handicapped children are well documented in the research literature and more recently some of the difficulties in using the Portage approach with such children have begun to emerge. Barna *et al.* (1980), reporting on the encouraging progress made by most children receiving the Portage home teaching service, mentioned that children with cerebral palsy and the visually handicapped group tended to develop at a very slow rate. Similarly, Bidder *et al.* (1982) reported that severely delayed children on their Portage scheme made fewest gains on the checklist. An even more depressing result was obtained by Felce *et al.* (1984) who found scarcely any evidence of skill acquisition in a group of profoundly handicapped adults in residential care who had received a modified Portage service.

This rather bleak picture which highlights the difficulties of teaching very severely and often multiply handicapped children is relieved a little by a number of recent initiatives which although still in their embryonic stages do offer exciting possibilities for this group. Such developments have occurred in the fields of curriculum planning, teaching method, assessment and evaluation and each of these is now discussed:

(a) Curriculum planning

Dessent and Ferguson (1984) have produced a comprehensive list of early teaching objectives in their checklist for the multiply handicapped. Although the task of selecting appropriate objectives for profoundly handicapped children remains a difficult one, materials such as these will aid this process and represent a useful downward extension of the existing Portage checklist produced by Bluma *et al.* (1976).

(b) Teaching method

The Portage activity chart is a highly sophisticated teaching method. These charts have a remarkably high success rate (Shearer and Shearer, 1972, Revill and Blunden, 1978, Castillo *et al.*, 1982), but even this can be improved.

A considerable amount of work is going on at present to clarify the essential variables in *teaching* the profoundly handicapped. Such research includes the presentation of materials in discrimination tasks (Remington *et al.*, 1981) and the selective use of rewards (Olenick and Pear, 1980). Pioneering work is also going on in developing *management* techniques for highly disruptive behaviour (Kushlick *et al.*, 1985, Lovass, 1985) and this work is not only demonstrating how it is possible to dramatically decrease disruptive behaviour but also to replace this with useful, appropriate new skills.

All of these research developments could be incorporated into a Portage activity chart to improve the effectiveness of teaching the profoundly handicapped child.

(c) Assessment

The Portage activity chart measures two pieces of assessment data – whether the learner carried out the response (a) without help or (b) with help. For children who find great difficulty in learning however it may be important also to look additionally at the *quality* of the desired behaviour.

As yet Portage does not have any systematic way of closely scrutinizing the performance of the learner. Such a device is however readily available in the Education of the Developmentally Young materials (EDY) developed at the University of Manchester (Foxen and McBrien, 1981) where the Qualitative Behaviour Record Schedule could easily be adapted for home teachers and parents on a Portage scheme.

(d) Evaluation

Another great strength of the EDY approach is that it allows the teacher to evaluate his or her performance using a Trainee Assessment Form. Systematic feedback of this type has tended to get overlooked on Portage yet when teaching profoundly handicapped children the performance of the teacher is a crucial element in the learning equation. Once again, the Trainee Assessment Form could easily be adapted for use on a home visit and would provide parents and home teachers with the kind of data which would enable them to teach even more effectively.

The development of new criterion referenced checklist materials and continued research into the finer aspects of teaching method are encouraging developments within the existing Portage model. At the same time the EDY approaches to providing feedback on both the performance of the learner and the teacher, could provide exciting new extensions to the existing Portage model (see Figure 3). Considering the degree of overlap which exists between Portage and EDY, it is scarcely surprising that 'the case for an arranged marriage' has been strongly made (see Stratford and Coyne, 1986, for a stimulating discussion of this possibility).

Early communication skills

Although the Portage approach has been successfully used to stimulate early language development, the selection and teaching of early language skills demands considerable care and these are tasks on which most home teachers are likely to want to involve other supporting professionals, particularly speech therapists. Recent research has begun to identify some specific problems in acquiring communication skills faced by children who have moderate and severe learning difficulties.

There are two major problem areas. In the first place, a number of researchers, notably Butterworth (1984), Dunst *et al*, (1982) and Smith (1983), have reported that many handicapped children have *specific difficulties* in acquiring general communication skills, particularly imitation behaviours. A second problem concerns the parents of handicapped children. There are some indications that parents may use functionally different language towards their handicapped child (Cardoso-Martins and Mervis, 1985) and are less likely to follow the child's initiative (Jones, 1980). A modest study reported by Vicary (1985) suggested that Portage parents tended (initially at least) to use more directive speech to their children than other parents of handicapped children.

These research findings lead us to ask two questions.

Figure 3: A model of Curriculum Management (after Lister and Cameron, 1986) showing how features of the Portage home teaching model and the Education of the Developmentally Young Project might be combined to produce an improved service for profoundly handicapped children.

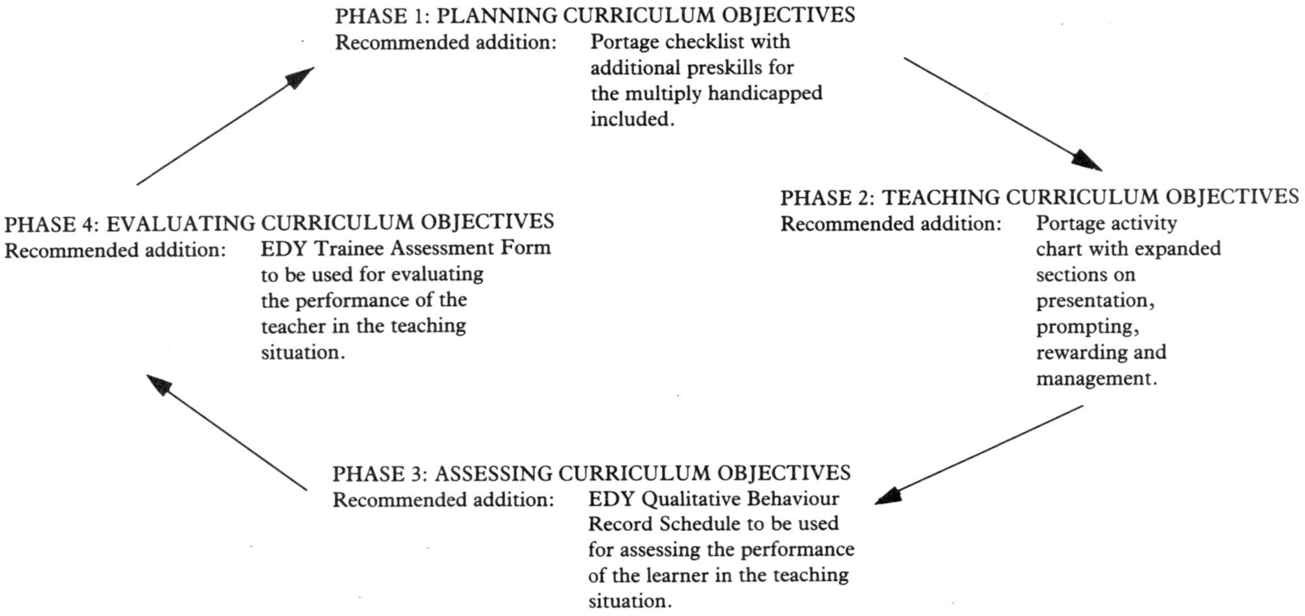

(a) Can children with special needs be helped to overcome some of their specific learning difficulties in early communication?
(b) Can Portage help parents of handicapped children to respond more appropriately to their child's developmental level in language?

At present neither of these questions has been answered but there are some promising initiatives already occurring in Portage. In 1983 White and East produced their revised version of the language section of the Portage checklist. The *Wessex Revised Portage Checklist* offers a number of advantages for both parents and children. A section on *adult behaviour* ensures that the parent responds appropriately to the child's level of language and provides the child with opportunities to develop existing language skills. As far as the child is concerned, the new checklist represents a considerably extended version of the original so that the selection of appropriate skills for teaching becomes easier. Many of these additional items fall into the category of *vocal and gestural imitation* which are precisely the specific deficit areas highlighted by research.

An important piece of additional research needs to be carried out to determine whether the finer grained objectives for children together with the more appropriate adult behaviours produce a significant improvement in childrens' early communication skills. At this stage, the possibility seems highly promising!

The quality of learning

> The criteria for writing activity charts are so precise that the outcome of the parents teaching is almost doomed to success (Cameron, 1979).

> We find the assumptions and principles of learning by Portage incompatible with the present knowledge of how children learn ... our task is therefore to find means whereby a child can be supported in his/her own search for understanding (Smith, 1984).

These two quotations highlight the essential differences between two often competing approaches in applied psychology – the *Cognitive* and *Behavioural* models. Both approaches have exerted a considerable influence in applied psychological research and tend to move in and out of fashion in psychology. (The dominant effect of the cognitive model in the 1960s began to give way to the more behaviourally-orientated 1970s and at the present time the cognitive model appears to be on the ascent once again.)

What is the essential difference between these two approaches? Cognitive psychologists attempt to study the mental functioning of an individual and are interested in processes like thinking, remembering, deducing, understanding, recognizing, perceiving, etc. This interest in 'within–person' variables has often been used to *explain* human behaviour.

Behavioural approaches on the other hand concentrate on the observable behaviour of individuals, i.e. what people say and do. Learning is seen as the central aspect of human development and teaching is viewed as the most important process. This emphasis on how people learn has meant that behavioural psychologists have concentrated on *changing* human behaviour.

Although these distinctions may seem very much like a private battle going on inside psychology (and to some extent this is true) the two approaches have generated different models of teaching and often made claims and counter claims about their effectiveness. Behavioural psychologists take a 'bottom-up' view of teaching and suggest that skills should be taught systematically and in sequence. The name given to such a teaching method is 'Direct Instruction' (DI) and Portage teaching has many elements of DI. The cognitive approach on the other hand could be described as 'top down' and concentrates on enhancing an individual's cognitive processes or teaching general problem solving strategies. The Instrumental Enrichment approach pioneered in Israel (Feurstein, 1985) is a good example of a teaching method which has its roots in cognitive psychology.

If we return to the two quotations at the beginning of this section, we can begin to redefine the question which they highlight as follows: 'Do Direct Instructional approaches like Portage lead to high quality learning?' Or, more crudely: 'Are Portage home teachers helping children to acquire *generalizable skills* or are they merely teaching them *tricks*?'

Unfortunately, there is no direct evidence of work carried out with pre-school handicapped children which we can use to resolve the question. However some attempts can be made to clarify the situation by examining the data from the US 'Follow through' project. This large-scale research project was aimed at reducing school failure among economically disadvantaged pupils and a total of 75,000 children in 170 communities took part, with more than 20 different approaches being evaluated. Reproduced in Table 3 is a considerably simplified comparison of just three of these educational approaches – the open classroom model (apparently based on the British infant school system!); the cognitively orientated curriculum model (partly based on the work of Piaget) and the Direct Instructional model (with its rationale in behavioural psychology).

The independent evaluation reported in Becker *et al.* (1981) (and in a number of other published papers) examined what were considered to be three important features of any compensatory educational programme:

(a) How well the programme succeeded in teaching basic scholastic skills especially reading, spelling and mathematics.
(b) How well the programme helped children to develop problem solving strategies which would enable them to *apply* basic skills.
(c) How the children themselves reacted to the teaching programme in terms of improved self-esteem.

Table 3: Project Follow through: comparison of three approaches to teaching economically disadvantaged children (extracted from Becker *et al.*, 1981)

Success rate	Basic skills	Problem solving	Affective measures
1st	Direct Instruction	Direct Instruction	Direct Instruction
2nd	———	———	———
3rd	———	———	———
4th	———	———	———
5th	———	———	Cognitively Orientated Curriculum
6th	———	———	———
7th	———	———	———
8th	Open Education	Cognitively Orientated Curriculum	———
9th	Cognitively Orientated Curriculum	Open Education	Open Education

NB: In the Becker *et al.* (1981) research write-up, a total of nine different teaching approaches were compared: only three are listed in this simplified table.

The results of this comparative study are both clear cut and convincing. Not only, as everyone expected, did DI approaches succeed best of all in teaching basic skills to children but (contrary to what was expected) the data also demonstrated that children on the DI programme could use these skills to solve new problems. In addition positive change occurred in the way in which children on the DI programme viewed themselves as individuals. In short, the Direct Instructional approach out-performed all the other teaching methods in terms of teaching basic skills, helping children to develop problem solving strategies and improving their self-esteem.

While the results of this large-scale study are most encouraging for people working within the Portage model, it is important to guard against complacency. As has been strongly argued at the Second National Portage Conference in Cambridge (Cameron, 1984a), the elements for ensuring that children learn to *generalize* and *adapt* the skills they have been taught on a teaching programme should always be built into the teaching programme. Generalization and adaptation should not merely be expected to occur naturally. Fortunately, in the Portage scheme, many features which lead to generalization and adaptation are already built into the model but some additional suggestions are made in the Cameron (*op. cit.*) paper.

One of the most important strategies for encouraging high quality learning was described by White (1986) at the Fourth National Portage Conference. She stressed the importance of *structured play* in helping children with special needs to maintain, generalize and adapt the skills they have been taught. Interestingly enough, the importance of structured play in teaching is also stressed by a number of people working within the cognitive model including Hewson *et al.* (1980), McConkey (1981) and Smith (1984).

Encouraging high quality learning is a future research growth area and because the Portage teaching system teaching approach has such solid foundations it can be easily built upon. Once again, a modest beginning has already been made!

Advanced training

The four topics which have taken up most of the content of this chapter are of course relatively new and only briefly touched upon in basic Portage training workshops. The need for an advanced Portage workshop for experienced Portage home teachers, supervisors and parents has been highlighted (Daly, 1984) and these topics – dealing with non-educational problems, teaching the profoundly handicapped child, teaching early communication skills and helping children to generalize and adapt taught skills – are likely to form the major part of this advanced curriculum.

Some conclusions

The success of the Portage home teaching scheme has had a positive effect on other educational services for pre-school handicapped children and many aspects of Portage, e.g. multi-agency collaboration, individualized educational programmes, individualized teaching and positive monitoring and recording have been taken up and adapted for use within other parts of the educational system. It is also clear from the points raised in this chapter that Portage has not just acted as an exemplary service but the model has shown itself robust enough to be adapted to new settings and different client groups. Portage has also developed and expanded into new problem areas and as a result has both stimulated research and identified new areas for future investigation. All of these have been used to improve and strengthen the original home teaching model.

Given the slow rate of change which is a feature of the UK educational scene, the growth of Portage services and technology can only be described as an impressive performance by a scheme which relies on parents, uses a minimum of professional time, utilizes no complex educational technology or materials, often operates at a fraction of the cost of other pre-school services and is only now celebrating its tenth anniversary!

Editors' note: R.J. Cameron's chapter is an appropriate final chapter in this book. The author takes us through an historical account of the Portage activities in the United States and the United Kingdom since 1969 and then looks in some detail at the criticisms that are levelled.

The expansion of Portage services around the country and into a variety of different settings inevitably brings new problems in its wake, but these in turn provide the stimulation and impetus for further research and problem solving. R.J. Cameron's chapter is an inspiration for us to go out and problem solve and continually to monitor and improve the range and quality of our service deliveries to families and children with special needs.

Appendix 1: The Portage home teaching model: a selection of US and UK research

Research phase	Questions asked	Date of study	Source of published data	Numbers taking part	Reported outcome of study
Implementation and early research US	Does the Portage home teaching service enhance the development of pre-school children with special needs?	1970 – 1971	Cochrane and Shearer (1984)	57 families	Children gained 18.3 IQ points over a 9-month period.
		1971 – 1972	Shearer and Shearer (1972)	75 families	Average child gained 13 months developmentally over 8-month period. Also 91% of activities taught by parents successfully attained by children.
		1973 – 1974	Cochrane and Shearer (1984)	130 families	Children had higher than predicted gains in self help, physical, social communication and academic develop-ment.
Implementation in UK	Can the Portage model be operated in the UK context and using exis-ting services?	May – Dec 1976	Smith *et al*. (1977)	13 families in Winchester	Child gains: 82% teaching objectives attained. Parent cooper-ation and satisfaction high.

		July – March 1977	Revill and Blunden (1979)	19 families in South Glamorgan	Child gains: 88% of teaching objectives attained. Rate of skill acquisition faster with Portage. More skills learned other than those directly taught.
Follow-up studies UK	Can the level of service be maintained?	June – Dec 1979	Castillo *et al.* (1982)	17 families in Winchester	Child gains: 92% of teaching objectives attained. Parent cooperation and satisfaction remained high.
		March – Dec 1977	Revill and Blunden (1978)	6 families in Dyfed	The study showed that the service could be replicated in a rural area of Wales using existing staff resources and with minimal research involvement.

Conclusion

Robin Hedderly and Kath Jennings

This book has covered a wide range of Portage topics. It has included chapters which have considered the very beginnings of Portage and it has also included chapters which have pointed to developments and extensions into schools and nursery schools, and indeed into other branches of the education service. R.J. Cameron's chapter has documented the rather brief history of Portage, particularly in the United Kingdom. It is difficult at this time to envisage the next ten years, for as R.J. Cameron remarks in the concluding chapter of this book, the people working within Portage have not only been able to maintain and add to the original service delivery model but they have expanded the technology into new problem areas. It is also interesting to notice that the Portage methodology has been incorporated into other branches of psychology and indeed even into other disciplines. The Portage methodology is extremely robust, and with its emphasis on evaluation and monitoring it has an important place as a basis for the delivery of all caring and support agencies.

It is clear with the technological developments in society that one of the major consequences in the westernized English-speaking world, is the development of 'service' industries. A Portage methodology is one in which enables 'capitalistic' service deliveries and 'socialistic' service deliveries to be offered in an efficient and human way. Perhaps within the next ten years we can look forward to the situation where the Portage service delivery model is used to evaluate all such service deliveries. This can contribute to helping the economy develop significantly because the Portage system offers direct help in a way which enables people to learn and to take responsibility for their own affairs whatever the disadvantage they may suffer. The Portage system also enables one to set tasks and targets, and the Portage methodology could make a useful contribution to the running of the welfare state in general.

At the moment, in many branches of the helping services we do not always know what it is we are trying to achieve. Even if we do know, we set such vague targets and imprecise objectives and unclear evaluation systems that we are very unsure as to whether we have achieved anything or not. The fact that people everywhere are frustrated by the bureaucracy and the systems that we set up in society is evidence indeed that somehow we have not always got it right. It has been mentioned in a number of chapters in this book that the Portage methodology is robust and adaptable. We would like to see more people applying the approach in a systematic and human as well as in a humane way. This is not always easy as the Kirklees psychological service has already found out.

We have made several attempts to adapt the Portage model to other branches of the psychological service. The people taking prime responsibility for children are not always keen to participate in such a tight evaluation system. It takes time for some people to find out that working in the Portage model is very rewarding and satisfying both for the demonstrators of the techniques and the recipients of the service. Just informing people that the method is good is not sufficient. One has to engage people actively in participating in the project. Convincing administrators is also extremely difficult; people do not want to change the way they are doing things already and often they do not receive an incentive to change. However there are many problems that society has currently to face. The problems of unemployment and of disaffected young people for example are current issues. The immense problem in agreeing what to teach pupils in our educational system and how to assess whether we succeed is one that we have to tackle. The Portage methodology may not help us agree a curriculum but at least it will offer a method of knowing whether we have achieved some of the goals that we set ourselves.

It is heartening to know that the National Portage Association is thriving and expanding. Those people who are initiated in the very beginning into the Portage methodology have been very pleased to receive praise from a wide range of people and places. It is to be hoped that the next ten years will see no bounds to the creativity of parents, professionals and administrators and the people in government. If this creativity can be used to develop and extend the Portage model even further in order to help and support children, parents and caring adults, in all walks of life then perhaps we can all look forward to a better world tomorrow.

References

AINSCOW, M. and TWEDDLE, D. (1984). *Early Learning Skills Analysis*. Chichester: John Wiley.

APLIN, G. and PUGH, G. (1983). *Perspectives on Pre-School Home Visiting*. London : National Children's Bureau.

ARNEY, S. and CONNOLLY, J. (1984). *Kirklees Portage Project: Evaluation*. Huddersfield: Kirklees Psychological Service.

BARNA, S., BIDDER, R.R., GRAY, O.P., CLEMENTS, J. and GARDNER, S. (1980). 'The progress of developmentally delayed pre-school children in a home training scheme', *Child: Care, Health and Development*, 6, 157–164.

BARSH, E.T., MOORE, J.A., and HAMMERLYNCK, L.A. (1983). 'The foster extended family: a social network for handicapped foster children', *Child Welfare*, 62, 349–359.

BECKER, W.C., ENGELMANN, S., CARNINE, D.W. and RHINE, W.R. (1981). 'Direct Instruction Model'. In: RHINE, W.R. (Ed) *Making Schools More Effective: New Directions from Follow Through*. New York: Academic Press.

BENDALL, S. (1985). 'National Portage Survey – preliminary results'. In: DALY, B., ADDINGTON, J., KERFOOT, S. and SIGSTON, A. (Eds) *Portage: The Importance of Parents*. Windsor: NFER-NELSON.

BIDDER, R.T., HEWITT, K.E. and GRAY, O.P. (1982). 'Evaluation of teaching method in a home-based training scheme for developmentally delayed pre-school children', *Child: Care Health and Development*, 9, 1–12.

BLUMA, S., SHEARER, M., FROHMAN, A., and HILLIARD, J. (1976). *Portage Guide to Early Education: Checklist*. Windsor: NFER-NELSON.

BLUNDEN, R. (1982). 'Tailored to suit', *Nursing Mirror*. Feb, 24.

BRONFENBRENNER, U. (1974). *Is Early Intervention Effective?* A report on longitudinal evaluations of preschool programmes. Vol. II. (DHEW Publication No. OHO 75–25). Washington, DC: US Dept. of Health, Education and Welfare.

BUCKLEY, S. (1984). 'The influence of family variables on children's progress on Portage'. In: DESSENT, T. (Ed) *What is Important about Portage?* Windsor: NFER-NELSON.

BURDEN, R.L. (1980). 'Measuring the effects of stress on the mothers of handicapped infants: must depression always follow?' *Child: Care, Health and Development*, 6, 111–125.

BUTTERWORTH, G. (1984). Cognitive Problems in Infancy. Paper presented to the 'Association pour la recherche sur l'autisme et la psychose infantile'. Paris, France (November).

CAMERON, J. (1984). 'A parent's view'. In: DESSENT, T. (Ed) *What is Important about Portage?* Windsor: NFER-NELSON.

CAMERON, R.J. (1979). 'A lot can happen at home too', *Remedial Education*, 14, 4, 173–178.

CAMERON, R.J. (Ed) (1982). *Working Together: Portage in the UK*. Windsor: NFER-NELSON.

CAMERON, R.J. (1984a). 'Extending Portage teaching: helping children to generalize and adapt taught skills'. In: DESSENT, T. (Ed) *What is Important about Portage?* Windsor: NFER-NELSON.

CAMERON, R.J. (1984b). 'Portage in the UK: 1984', *Journal of Community Education*, 3, 3, 24–33.

CAMERON, R.J. (1985). 'A problem centred approach to family problems'. In: DALY, B., ADDINGTON, J., KERFOOT, S. and SIGSTON, A. (Eds) *Portage: The Importance of Parents*. Windsor: NFER-NELSON.

CAMERON, R.J. (1986). 'Who pays for Portage?' In: BISHOP, M., COPLEY, M. and PORTER, J. (Eds) *Portage: More Than a Teaching Programme?* Windsor: NFER-NELSON.

CAMERON, R.J., CHAMBERS, G. and MARTIN, S. (1984). 'What is wrong with Portage?' *Health Visitor*, 57, 142–144.

CARDOSO-MARTINS, C. and MERVIS, C.B. (1985). 'Maternal speech to pre-linguistic children with Down's syndrome', *American Journal of Mental Deficiency*, 89, 5, 451–458.

CARR, J. (1975). *Young Children with Down's Syndrome*. IRRMH Monograph No. 4. London: Butterworth.

CASTILLO, M., SMITH, J., GLOSSOP, C. and KUSHLICK, A. (1982). The Wessex Portage Project: Maintenance after Three Years. Research Report No. 154. University of Southampton: Wessex Health Care and Evaluation Research Team.

CLAYTON, T. (1985). 'The workshop approach to training behavioural skills', *Education and Child Psychology*, 2, 1, 69–83.

CLEMENTS, J., EVANS, C., JONES, C., OSBORNE, K. and UPTON, G. (1981). *The Development and Evaluation of an Assessment-linked Training Scheme for the Mentally Handicapped Child*. St Cadoc's Hospital, Gwent: Psychology Department.

CLEMENTS, J., SMITH, J., SPAIN, B. WATKEYS, J. (1982). 'A preliminary investigation on the use of Portage systems in day nursery settings', *Child: Care Health and Development*, 8, 123–131.

COCHRANE, D.C. and SHEARER, D.E. (1984). 'The Portage model for home teaching'. In: PAINE, S.C., BELLAMY, G.T., and WILCOX, B. (Eds) *Human Services that Work*. Baltimore, MD: Brookes Publishing Company.

COURT, S.D.M. (Chairperson) (1976). *Fit for the Future*. Report of the Committee of Child Health Services. Cmnd 6684. London: HMSO.

CULLEN, S.M., CRONK, C.E., PUESCHEL, S.M., SCHNELL, R.R. and REED, R.B. (1981). 'Social development and feeding milestones of young Down's syndrome infants', *American Journal of Mental Deficiency*, 85, 410–415.

CUNNINGHAM, C.C. and SLOPER, P. (1978). *Helping Your Handicapped Child*. London: Souvenir Press.

CUSWORTH, S. (1980). Kirklees pre-pilot Portage project: an evaluation. Unpublished document. Huddersfield: Kirklees Psychological Service.

DALY, B. (1984). 'Report on the work of the National Portage Association Training and Monitoring Committee', *Portage Post*, 1, 6.

DAVIS, H. (1985). 'Developing the role of parent advisor in the child health services. In: DE'ATH, E. and PUGH, G. (Eds) *Partnership Paper 3*. London: National Children's Bureau.

DEPARTMENT OF HEALTH AND SOCIAL SECURITY (1969). Report of the Committee of Inquiry into Allegations of Ill-Treatment of Patients and other Irregularities at the Ely Hospital, Cardiff. Cmnd 3975. London: HMSO.

DEPARTMENT OF HEALTH AND SOCIAL SECURITY (1978). Report of the Committee of Inquiry into Normansfield Hospital. Cmnd 7357. London: HMSO.

DEPARTMENT OF HEALTH AND SOCIAL SECURITY (1979). Report of the Committee of Inquiry into Mental Handicap Nursing and Care (Jay Report). Cmnd 7468. London: HMSO.

DEPARTMENT OF HEALTH AND SOCIAL SECURITY (1980). Mental Handicap: Progress Problems and Priorities. A review of the mental handicap services in England since the 1971 White Paper Better Services for the Mentally Handicapped. London: HMSO.

DEPARTMENT OF HEALTH AND SOCIAL SECURITY (1984). *Helping Mentally Handicapped People with Special Problems*. London: HMSO.

DESSENT, T. (Ed) (1984). *What is Important about Portage?* Windsor: NFER-NELSON.

DESSENT, S. and FERGUSON, L. (1984). 'First encounters with the multiply handicapped'. In: DESSENT, T. (Ed) *What is Important about Portage?* Windsor: NFER-NELSON.

DE SOUSA, D. (1985). 'Evaluating a short in-service course'. *Education and Child Psychology*, 2, 1, 83–90.

DUMAS, J.E. and WAHLER, R.G. (1983). 'Predictions of treatment outcome in parent training: mother insularity and socio-economic disadvantage', *Behavioural Assessment*, 5, 301–313.

DUNST, C.J., BRASSEL, W.R. and RHEINGROVER, R.M. (1982). 'Structural and organisational features of sensori-motor intelligence among retarded infants and toddlers', *British Journal of Educational Psychology*, 51, 133–143.

FELCE, D. and DE KOCK, U. (1983). *Planning Client Activity: A Handbook*. University of Southampton: Health Care Evaluation Research Team.

FELCE, D., DE KOCK, U., MANSELL, J. and JENKINS, J. (1984). 'Providing systematic individual teaching for severely disturbed and profoundly handicapped mentally handicapped adults in residential care', *Behaviour Research and Therapy*, 22, 3, 299–309.

FEUERSTEIN, R. with RAND, Y. and HOFFMAN, M.B. (1985). *Instrumental Enrichment: an Intervention Programme for Cognitive Modifiability*. Baltimore, MD: University Park Press.

FOXX, R.M. and AZRIN, N.H. (1972). 'Restitution: a method of eliminating aggressive-disruptive behaviour of retarded and brain damaged patients', *Behaviour Research and Therapy*, 10, 15–27.

FOXX, R.M. and AZRIN, N.H. (1977). *Toilet Training the Retarded: A Program for Day and Night Time Independent Toiletting*. Champaign, Ill: Research Press.

FOXX, R.M. and LIVESAY, J. (1984). 'Maintenance of response suppression following overcorrection: a 10 year retrospective examination of eight cases', *Analysis and Intervention in Developmental Disabilities*, 65–79.

FOXEN, T. and MCBRIEN, J. (1981). *The EDY Inservice Course for Mental Handicap Practitioners: Training Staff in Behavioural Methods.* (a) Instruction Handbook, (b) Trainee Workbook. Manchester: University Press.

GEIGER, W.L., BROWNSMITH, K. and FORGNONE, C. (1978). 'Differential importance of skills for TMR students as perceived by teachers', *Education and Training of the Mentally Retarded*, 13, 259–264.

GOODMAN, J.F., CECIL, H.S. and BARKER, W.F. (1984). 'Early interaction with retarded children: some encouraging results', *Developmental Medicine and Childhood Neurology*, 26, 47–55.

GRAY, S.W., RAMSEY, B.K. and KLAUS, R.A. (1982). *From Three to Twenty: The Early Training Project*. Baltimore, MD: University Park Press.

GRAY, S.W. and WANDERSON, L.P. (1980). 'The methodology of home based intervention studies', *Child Development*, 51, 993–1009.

GRIEST, D.L., FOREHAND, R. and WELLS, K.C. (1981). 'Follow up assessment of parental behavioural training', *Child Study Journal*, 11, 221–229.

HEBDEN, H. and WHYTE, R. (1983). *Developmental Progress Charts*. Blackburn: 72 Preston New Road.

HEBER, R. and GARBER, H. (1975). 'The Milwaukee Project. A study of the use of family intervention to prevent cultural familial mental retardation'. In: FRIEDLANDER, B., STERRIT, G. and KIRK, G., (Eds) *Exceptional Infant, Vol.3*. New York: Brunner/Mazell.

HEDDERLY, R. (1977). 'Contract based referral system: the way to a community psychological service?' *Association of Educational Psychologists' Journal*, 4, 5, 15–20.

HEDDERLY, R. (1980). 'Memory banks, data banks and confidentiality', *Bulletin of the British Psychological Society*, 33, 121–123.

HEWSON, S., McCONKEY, R. and JEFFREE, D. (1980). 'The relationship between structured and free play in the development of a mentally handicapped child: a case study', *Child: Care, Health and Development*, 6, 2, 73–82.

HOLLAND, F.L.U. and NOAKS, J.C. (1982). 'Portage in Mid-Glamorgan: description and comment on this pre-school home intervention scheme', *Journal of the Association of Educational Psychologists*, 5, 9, 32–37.

JONES, O.H.M. (1980). 'Prelinguistic communication skills in Down's syndrome and normal infants'. In: FIELD, T.M. (Ed) *High Risk Infants and Children: Adult and Peer Interactions*. New York: Academic Press.

KOEGEL, R.L., GLAN, T.J. and NIEMINEN, G. (1978). 'Generalization of parent-training results', *Journal of Applied Behaviour Analysis*, 11, 95–109.

KOEGEL, R.L., RUSSO, D.C. and RINCOVER, A. (1977). 'Assessing and training teachers in the generalized use of behaviour modification with autistic children', *Journal of Applied Behaviour Analysis*, 10, 197–205.

KUSHLICK, A. and COX, G.R. (1973). 'The epidemiology of mental handicap', *Develop. Med. Child. Neurol.*, 15, 748–759.

KUSHLICK, A., SMITH, J. and GOLD, A. (1985). 'An intervention package to teach parents of severely retarded and severely non-compliant children and adults at home to teach their children new relevant skills'. In: DALY, B., ADDINGTON, J., KERFOOT, S. and SIGSTON, A. (Eds) *Portage: the Importance of Parents*. Windsor: NFER-NELSON.

LE POIDEVIN, S. and CAMERON, J. (1985). 'Is there more to Portage than education?' In: DALY, B., ADDINGTON, J., KERFOOT, S. and SIGSTON, A. (Eds) *Portage: the Importance of Parents*. Windsor: NFER-NELSON.

LE POIDEVIN, S. (1986). 'Bereavement counselling'. In: BISHOP, M., COPLEY, M. and PORTER, J. (Eds) *Portage: More Than a Teaching Programme?* Windsor: NFER-NELSON.

LISTER, T.A.J. (1985). 'Portage – eight years on'. In: DALY, B., ADDINGTON, J., KERFOOT, S. and SIGSTON, A. (Eds) *Portage: the Importance of Parents*. Windsor: NFER-NELSON.

LISTER, T.A.J. and CAMERON, R.J. (1986). 'Curriculum management (Part 1): Planning curriculum objectives', *Educational Psychology in Practice*, 2, 1, 6–14.

LOVAAS, O.I. (1985). Behavioural treatment and recovery in young autistic children. Unpublished interim research report. Los Angeles: University of California.

LOVAAS, O.I., ACKERMAN, A., ALEXANDER, D., FIRESTONE, P., PERKINS, M. and YOUNG, D.B. (1981). *Teaching Developmentally Disabled Children – The ME Book*. Baltimore MD: University Park Press.

LOVETT, H. (1985) *Cognitive Counselling for Persons with Special Needs*. Connecticut: Praeger.

McCAIL, G. (1981). *Mother Start.* Edinburgh: Scottish Council for Research in Education.

McCONKEY, R. and GALLAGHER, F. (1984). *Lets Play.* University of Ulster and St Michaels House.

McMAHON, R.J., FOREHAND, R. and GRIEST, D.L. (1981). 'Effect of knowledge of social learning principles on enhancing treatment outcome and generalization in a parent training programme', *Journal of Clinical and Consulting Psychology*, 49, 526–532.

OLENICK, D.L. and PEAR, J.P. (1980). 'Differential reinforcement of correct responses to probes and prompts in picture name training with severely retarded children,' *Journal of Applied Behavior Analysis*, 13, 77–89.

OLIVER, C., MURPHY, G.H. and CORBETT, J.A. (1985). *The Epidemiology of Self-Injurious Behaviour in People with Mental Handicap.* Croydon: Hilda Lewis House.

OSBORN, A. (1984). *The Social Life of Britain's Five Year Olds.* London: Routledge and Kegan Paul.

PHILPS, C. (1984). *Elizabeth Joy: a mother's story.* Tring, Herts: Lion Publishing.

PRIESTLY, M. and McGUIRE, J. (1983). *Learning to Help.* London: Tavistock.

PRINGLE, M.K. *et al.* (1980). *A Fairer Future for Children: Towards Better Parental and Professional Care.* London: Macmillan, on behalf of the National Children's Bureau.

PUGH, G. (1981) *Parents as Partners: Intervention Schemes and Group Work with Parents of Handicapped Children.* London: National Children's Bureau.

PUGH, G. and DE'ATH, E. (1984). *The Needs of Parents.* London: Macmillan.

PUGH, G. and RUSSELL, P. (1977). *Shared Care: Support Services for Families with Handicapped Children.* London: National Children's Bureau.

READER, L. (1984). 'Review pre-school interaction programmes', *Child: Care, Health and Development*, 10, 237–251.

REMINGTON, B., LIGHT, P. and PORTER, D. (1981). 'A comparison of two methods of training symbol-object matching skills in non-speaking severely mentally retarded children', *Behaviour Research of Severe Developmental Disabilities*, 2, 157–174.

RENNIE, E.F.N. (1983). 'Evaluating Portage: a consideration of possibilities', *Community Education*, 3.

RENNIE, E.F.N. and JOYCE, J. (1979). 'Developing a data bank', *Bulletin of the British Psychological Society*, 32, 281–282.

REVILL, S. and BLUNDEN, R. (1978). *Home Training of Preschool Children with Developmental Delay.* Report of the development and evaluation of the replication of the Portage service in Ceredigion Health District, Dyfed. Research Report No. 5. Cardiff: Mental Handicap in Wales – Applied Research Unit.

REVILL, S. and BLUNDEN, R. (1979). 'A home training service for preschool developmentally handicapped children', *Behaviour Research and Therapy*, 17, 3, 207–214.

RUSSELL, P. (1985).'Portage – partnership with parents'. In: DALY, B., ADDINGTON, J., KERFOOT, S. and SIGSTON, A. (Eds) *Portage: the Importance of Parents*. Windsor: NFER-NELSON.

RUTTER, M., TIZARD, J. and WHITMORE, K. (1970). *Education, Health and Behaviour*. London: Longman.

SANDOW, S. (1984). 'The Portage project: ten years on'. In: DESSENT, T. (Ed) *What is Important about Portage?*. Windsor: NFER-NELSON.

SANDOW, S. and CLARKE, A.D.B. (1978). 'Home intervention with parents of severly subnormal pre-school children: an interim report', *Child: Care, Health and Development*, 4, 29–39.

SANDOW, S., CLARKE, A.D.B., COX, M.V. and STEWART, F.L. (1981). 'Home intervention with parents of severely subnormal pre-school children: A final report', *Child: Care, Health and Development*, 7, 135–144.

SHEARER, M.S. and SHEARER, D.E. (1972). 'The Portage Project: a model for early childhood education', *Exceptional Children*, 39, 3, 210–217.

SHINMAN, S. (1981). *A Chance for Every Child*. London:Tavistock.

SLOPER, P. (1983). 'Parental reaction to early intervention with their Down's Syndrome infants', *Child: Care, Health and Development*, 9, 357–376.

SMITH, C. (1983). A social cognitive approach to developmental handicap: beyond Portage. Paper presented at London Conference of British Psychological Society (December).

SMITH, C. (1984). Intervention groups for handicapped infants and their parents. Unpublished discussion paper. Southampton: Paediatric Department, Southampton General Hospital.

SMITH, G. (Ed) (1975). *Educational Priority Vol. 4. The West Riding Project*. London: HMSO.

SMITH, J., KUSHLICK, A. and GLOSSOP, C. (1977). *The Wessex Portage Project: A Home Teaching Service for Families with a Pre-school Mentally Handicapped Child*. Research Report No. 125. Part I: Report; Part II: Appendices. University of Southampton: Wessex Health Care and Evaluation Research Team.

SPECK, R. and ATTNEAVE, C. (1973). *Family Networks*. New York: Poulton Books.

STRATFORD, R.J. and COYNE, G. (1986). 'EDY meets Portage: the case for an arranged marriage', *Educational Psychology in Practice*, 2, 2 (in press).

THOMSON, C., HOLMBERG, M. and BAER, D. (1978). 'An experimental analysis of some procedures to teach priming and reinforcement skills to pre-school teachers', *Monographs of the Society for Research in Child Development*, 43, 4.

TIZARD, B. and HUGHES, M. (1984). *Young Children Learning*. London: Fontana.

TIZARD, B., MORTIMORE, J. and BURCHELL, B. (1981). *Involving Parents in Nursery and Infant Schools*. London: Grant McIntyre.

TURNBULL, A.P. and TURNBULL, H.R. (1982). 'Parent involvement in the education of handicapped children: a critique', *Mental Retardation*, 20.

VAN DER EYKEN, W. (1982). *Homestart: A Four Year Evaluation*. Leicester: Leicester Homestart Consultancy.

VICARY, S. (1985). 'Observations of mothers interacting with their developmentally delayed one-year-olds'. In: DALY, B., ADDINGTON, J., KERFOOT, S. and SIGSTON, A. (Eds) *Portage: The Importance of Parents*. Windsor: NFER-NELSON.

WALTERS, J., DAVIES, M., DALE, P. and MORRISON, T. (1984). *Family-Agency Networks*. Rochdale: NSPCC.

WARNOCK, M. (Chairperson) (1978). *Special Educational Needs*. Report of the Committee of Inquiry into the education of handicapped children and young people. Cmnd 7212 London:HMSO.

WEBSTER, D.R. and AZRIN, N.H. (1973). 'Required relaxation: a method of inhibiting agitative disruptive behaviour of retardates', *Behavior Research and Therapy*, 11, 67–78.

WEEKS, R. and L'ABATE, L. (1982). *Paradoxical Psychotherapy: Theory and Practice with Individual Couples and Families*. New York: Brunner/Mazel.

WESTMACOTT, E. and CAMERON, R. (1981). *Behaviour Can Change*. Hampshire: Globe Education.

WHITE, M. (1986)'Educating the young child: support for the parent as teacher' In: BISHOP, M., COPLEY, M. and PORTER, J. (Eds) *Portage: More Than a Teaching Programme?* Windsor: NFER-NELSON.

WHITE, M. and EAST, K. (1983). *The Wessex Revised Portage Language Checklist*. Windsor: NFER-NELSON.

WISHART, M.C., BIDDER, R. and GRAY, O. (1980). 'Parental responses to their developmentally delayed children and the South Glamorgan home advisory service', *Child: Care, Health and Development*, 6, 361–376.

WOLFENDALE, S. (1985). 'Involving parents in assessment'. In: DE'ATH, E. and PUGH, G. (Eds) *Partnership Paper 3*. London: National Children's Bureau.